When Life Gives You Lemons... At Least You Won't Get Scurvy!

by
Madge Madigan

Copyright © 2013 Madge Madigan
All rights reserved.
ISBN: **1470199688**
ISBN-13: **978-1470199685**

2

Acknowledgments

My children Jack, Libby, and Abby for showing me what love is all about and for being so magnificent.

My Mother for being so amazing and feisty. My Father for laughing at my jokes. I sure miss you.

Tony for being there and motivating me to live up to my potential.

My siblings Kathy, Molly, Mike, Tom, and Jane for always being there for me.

Wendy Corsi Staub for her wonderful encouragement and guidance.

Vickijo Campanaro for all her encouragement and support.

Special thanks to: Lisa Balzer, Deborah Blizzard, Jill Sweeney-Bosa, Beth Brockett, Catherine Delia, Jeff Guilbert, Jeff Hansen, Anita Henderson, Geoff Lee, Andrew Nielsen, Gates Orlando, Bev DeSanto Rosen, Toby Shoemaker, Dana Snyder, Sara Tartaglia, Jack Zabelny

4

Contents

1. Change.............................. 6

2. Raising Children..................... 26

3. Finances............................ 48

4. Relationships....................... 67

5. Job/No Job......................... 83

6. Identity............................ 101

1. CHANGE

This book is broken down into 6 subjects. These subjects seem to be the major categories that we as adults find ourselves at odds with from time to time. Change, Raising Children, Finances, Relationships, Job/No Job, Identity.

This first chapter deals with a little more depressing material than the others... stay with me, it gets more amusing. Plenty of off-color jokes in future chapters. No, no don't skip ahead, this stuff is important. And this is the point, whether you like it or not we have to deal with the not so pleasant stuff in life, so un-knot your panties and just deal with it.

I got married in 1991. My children were born in 1994, 1997, and 1999. I got divorced in 2000. My brother-in-law Kevin died in 2004. My ex-husband skipped town and cut off ties in 2009. My oldest child went off to college in 2012. My Father passed away in 2012. My ex-husband tried to re-enter the kid's lives in 2013. Those were some pretty major changes in my life.

Changes can bring the highest highs or the lowest lows. Other than death and taxes, change is another certainty. People will come into the world, people will leave this world. Hearts will fall in love, hearts will get broken. Whatever the events bring, they are what shape us, make us who we are, for better or worse. It's how we deal with these events that make all the difference.

My divorce was a major bone crushing blow for me; it took me years to figure out who I was again because before that everything was apparently a big lie. I wrote these essays when I was finally turning a corner and trying to move on from the hurt and anger. I thought I had turned the corner several times before but this time I seemed to be more focused. It turns out getting yourself right is a series of corner-turns.

I started writing in 2005 to cope with my divorce, raising three kids mostly on my own, the new world of dating, and to try and find myself again. I started by writing a blog on MySpace. Yes, MySpace.

Then MySpace started to fall off the "cool meter" in 2009 or so. So the blogging waned. And then I got busy with kids, a relationship, trying a new career, and quite frankly I gained a more positive outlook and had fewer things to bitch about in a blog. (Which is mostly what my MySpace blog was about) I started writing in a new direction a year later. These are my changes.

Let the New Writing and Life Begin...

So, I'm on a mission. I think I've figured this out. The last couple of years I have been floundering with my writing. Wondering how to still be funny but with less raunch, more purpose to appeal to the masses. I have been trying to decide which direction to take, what focus I'd like to have. In essence I've been wanting to re-brand myself. Not like with a hot iron branding, marketing branding.

My MySpace blog years ago (to which I had a rather large following) was focused mostly on my dating and parenting life post-divorce. That was pretty easy since I hadn't been in a relationship for years. But really, how long can you write about that? It gets old after a while. Besides, my kids are teens now, I don't want them reading my dating exploits, and I'm sure it would be a major creep factor for them.

Think, think, think. What else do I know about? Well, it kind of hit me today... I know about survival. For those of you who know me, know that I have had quite a struggle over the past eleven years, well ok 20 years. For those of you who don't, here's a not entirely brief synopsis:

I thought I married a really nice, well educated, successful engineer and ex-Division I hockey player in 1991. But in 2000, I got out of a marriage to an eventual verbally abusive, alcoholic man, who had an affair on me while I was pregnant with our third child. Well back up a little, after a job transfer moved us from NY to Denver in 2000, where I didn't know a soul and had three children ages 6, 3, and 14 months, we divorced and he quickly moves in with the girl he had an affair with. He buys them a home and starts spending all his money on the two of them. I'm stuck to find whatever rental I can afford.

I had to keep finding jobs where I could take care of my children 90% of the time because he always travelled with his job. I had been a stay at home mom for 5 years; I could only get crap jobs. I was in radio and TV before that. I had to quit before I got fired because I'd have childcare problems. In 2004 he moved back East, leaving me in Denver to raise them alone, making monthly visits, which towards the end were cut short with kids calling me crying because Dad was drunk or passed out.

I was a realtor at the time and the bust hit Denver in 2006. I could no longer afford to live there and I was losing my mind raising the children alone who weren't quite old enough to be left alone yet. So I moved back to Rochester, NY at the end of

2006 with the promise from my ex that there would be all kinds of help from him and his parents. I started over, trying to find jobs, etc. Things were looking up after about a year, I decided to go back to school while working a decent job, then my ex went off the deep end. He sunk deep into his alcoholism and disappeared, skipped town, stopped paying support, stopped talking to the kids and me. The children were devastated. He did have his moments of being a good Dad, and they missed that.

I had to stop taking classes as I was on mental overload. My plans for advancement thwarted again. I felt I needed to find a new job because it was a half hour drive and I couldn't be that far from my kids with no other help, and I knew my employer wasn't happy with me because I was a mess, quite honestly. Well, they caught wind of me wanting/needing to leave and let me go or they forced me to quit or whatever. I was having a nervous breakdown. First I lost half my income with losing child support, then I was jobless, I was left with a pile of extra bills he was supposed to be paying (braces, sports, etc.) got evicted, had to apply for food stamps, Medicaid, free lunch at school, and clean friend's toilets to get gas money. There was even a point where I had absolutely no income before I got approved for aid that was a complete nightmare. But I did lose 20 lbs. from not being able to afford food! Hollah! (Important Tip: always look for silver lining- when life gives you lemons, at least you won't get scurvy)

Blah, blah, blah, there were many years before that of having to rescue my kids from torturous behaviour by their Dad that I won't even go into. Eventually I collected myself, got a few part-time jobs, then after a couple years re-directed myself into resuming my marketing career, and worked my way up to finding a full-time contract job (no benefits). My kids are thriving; they are all A students, and active in sports and music/theatre. My oldest is a senior and has applied to some of the best colleges in the country. I got financial aid all by myself for my kids to go to two of the best schools in the area, because they had the grades and drive to go. And amazingly we've talked our way through this and stuck together and have all remained well grounded. Nobody has started acting out, not even me. Ok, well I couldn't have gotten through this without cocktails now and then, but I'm an adult, I'm allowed. And most importantly friends and family, couldn't have made it through without them either. Oh and one other thing, I didn't seek out a man to save me. Although, a few years and pounds ago, that stripper pole was looking like it could be a way to eat.

So, why the long story? (What's sad is that I left a whole bunch of stuff out) To give you background on what I know. How to survive. My writing will be about how to survive adulthood. I will touch on all the adult subjects: financial, emotional, parenting, dating/relationships, jobs. I don't have all the answers, but I can share my experiences and tips for making it through some tough spots, all with a little laughter. Because really, humor makes it all bearable. At the very least, let my life serve as an example of what mistakes not to make.

That Time Steve Nash Stuck His Hand Up My Skirt...

Ok, so it hasn't been all seven plagues in the life of Madge. I have had a few laughs, smiles, and adventures in my life. Here's an interesting story, yet maybe something to be gleaned from it as well...

I lived in Denver from 2000 to 2006. I became a divorcee' in 2000. I had a few crazy years after my divorce. My heart was broken and I had been brainwashed into thinking I was a loser. I had to find myself again. Eventually I found a few other divorced Moms in my squeaky clean suburb that actually weren't Stepford Wives and wanted to have a little fun. Hey I was in my mid-30s, I wasn't dead yet!

In 2005 the NBA All-Star Game came to Denver. Now, I could give a rat's ass about pro basketball (except if maybe the Knicks were in the finals... which is like finding a unicorn) but it was probably a once in a lifetime chance to take in the spectacle. I decided to go downtown, I think it was maybe the night before the game; no it couldn't have been... I don't know it was one night of the All-Star weekend where they had activities going on. Several bars had special events, promising possible appearances of 2nd rate players, and there was one big event called the NBA Experience somewhere. We just wanted to see what was going on.

I had a friend, oh let's call her "Tanya". Now Tanya was a total MILF in her early 30s from my burb who made jaws drop when she walked in a room and she knew it. She nipped and tucked her body into a lovely va va voom silhouette. She was blonde haired and blue eyed and just oozed sexiness. She was very Marilyn-esque. "Tanya" dragged me along to some club that was supposed to be hot that night. Again, we weren't dead but we were in our 30s and downtown was filled with hot 20 somethings looking for an NBA player to rope into Baby-Daddy land. I reluctantly went in...

It was crowded and annoying. Some young drunk idiots were hitting on us; I was not interested in babysitting that night. Tanya was on the prowl. But she was a little bored with the youngins, so she gets on her bat phone. She thinks there is better action at this NBA Experience place. We haul our behinds over there via 16th St. tram. Crickets. The place was dead.

Tanya is back on the phone. We get back on the tram. We go to some other bar. She keeps holding my hand to walk me through the crowd; apparently this is something hot chicks do to tease the gentleman that they might be up for a threesome. I'm like damnit, quit grabbing my hand, you're not my Mother and I'm just not up for hot girl on girl action! Geez! That place was just kind of average, so Tanya's back on the phone. If you haven't noticed, she has a short attention span.
 Suddenly she tells me we're going to a bar I know well... but it's like this quiet wine bar/restaurant. I think to myself, "What the hell could be happening there?" Well whatever, I'm glad to get away from all the nightclub douchiness.

We get to the place, greeted outside by some guy that had apparently been on the other end of the phone with her all night, and the place is empty. It appears closed. However the dude assures us he is friends with the owner and he told us to come. Finally the owner does come to the door, greets the dude with hugs and tells us to come on back. I was thinking I just wanted to go home at that point. But we walk into the back room and there is a small (very small, about 10 people) party going on. Glasses of wine and scotch and cigars being smoked. We say hello, and the people barely gave us a nod. Then as I'm sitting there I realized who two of the men were. Thanks to my ex-husband's incessant sports watching, I realize the two men were Steve Nash and Dirk Nowitzki, teammates from the Dallas Mavericks, however Steve had just gone back to the Phoenix Suns at the time. I tried to keep my jaw from dropping. Tanya had no clue, I think the dude knew but I was oblivious to him anyway.

I didn't want to seem annoying and star struck, so I was polite, made small talk when possible. Steve is from Canada, so we chatted about me growing up near the border. Steve was a little bit of a cranky drunk though, and I think he was waiting for the "talent" to arrive. Dirk was just an out and out surly drunk. He was sitting there yelling obscenities and throwing crap, and laughing occasionally. In my head I so wanted to ask him to say "I must break you", but I figured he'd pick me up and throw me if I did.

Some Canadian old boys of Steve's finally showed up and they all piled on each other. It was a homie love fest. And with them arrived the "talent". A couple of 20 somethings in short plaid school girl skirts and high heels. I think they were off-duty strippers. They weren't there to perform necessarily, but they were there to look at and flirt. Mind you, I was wearing a short skirt and heels myself, but these chicks looked ya' know, ready for action.

It was time for the soccer moms to go. I knew we were just extra baggage, so I summoned Tanya to go. But we had to trek somewhere else in Denver to find our car. Steve and another guy said they were getting in their limo to go wherever and they would give us a ride to our car. Hey, ok we'll take it. We all pile in the limo, it was crowded, the trollops were sitting on the guy's laps. We get to our destination and all the men were very polite and said nice to meet you and... Steve is still seated with a girl on his lap and goes to help me out, I think, and all the sudden as I step out, his hand goes up my inner thigh!

Then the door quickly closed and they were off. I was a little shell shocked for a minute. Was it an accident? Or did I just get groped by an NBA All-Star? I was shocked, but I laughed. I think it was an accident or just a boy being a boy. A good number of other bottom feeder women would have tried to turn that into a money making situation. Now if perhaps he had palmed my privates while there, I probably would have called the police. But a harmless leg touch, however close it was to my no fly zone... I couldn't drag some harmless drunk dude through the mud with a dumb lawsuit where I was just trying to make a buck.

Maybe that's why I'm always broke, I'm not an opportunist. Should I be? Some people think I'm bitter, but I'm really not. I prefer the term curmudgeonly, but I'm not vindictive. I just don't have it in me to create senseless hurt for others.

Hopefully karma pays me back with a column or book contract or at least a lottery win!

This Wasn't the "Meeting in the Ladies Room" Klymaxx Envisioned...

Well, I survived the last couple of weeks with my 2 daughter's surgeries and my son's high school graduation. Piece of cake. Well, actually I think it's like child birth, there is some magic chemical in our bodies that makes us forget what hell we went through.

I got some interesting stories out of it, though. One in particular that happened to me sticks out though as a foreshadowing of my future... that I'll try to avoid as I transition from young Mother to eventual empty nester.

My son went to an all- boys Catholic prep school. So as part of any good Catholic high school graduation, they have a baccalaureate mass earlier in the day before graduation. My son had to get there early because he was singing at the mass with the school choir... and so we could get a seat, you know with us Catholics and our large families, seating was limited.

So, yea the mass... We had plenty of time to mill about and at one point my youngest daughter and I decide to go to the ladies room. (oh great now I have Klymaxx's "Meeting in the Ladies Room" stuck in my head) This particular ladies room had a long narrow, oh what would you call it, ya' know "lounge" with a sink and vanity and long counter for doing prissy lady things. I lovingly refer to it as the "pre-toilet" room. Then there is a one-seater toilet room beyond this room. My daughter and I are in line behind one other woman. This "lounge" room is long and narrow, so you all have to stand in line for the loo up against the wall like a police line-up.

The toilet room door opens and a cheery older woman comes out who is about in her 70s. The woman ahead of us goes in the toilet room. Older woman is chatting away "Oh sorry to hold everyone up!". This woman was probably one of the boy's Grandmas. She was wearing one of those "skirt suits" that old ladies wear with a skirt, an elaborately embroidered long jacket and rayon shell underneath, with a nice pair of sensible dress shoes and lots of diamond jewelry. As she's walking out she's tugging at her skirt and chatting away. I chatted back to be friendly as I always do. My kids actually said they like that I can make friendly conversation with anyone from a cashier to a nasty DMV clerk. Which is surprising because my parents did it when I was a kid and it used to embarrass the crap out of me. "Jesus Mary and Joseph, Mom! Do you have to talk to everyone, can't we just go?"

Right, so anyway, old lady comes out tugging and chatting, and then stops at the end of the counter space and is still chatting at me. Due to the specs of the room, there was nowhere to look but directly at her. She starts telling us that she got out quickly so as to let us all get in there and thought she would just adjust herself out in this particular area. Well thanks for explaining lady, I thought perhaps you had crazed weasels up your skirt or something. She chats more (for the life of me I can't remember the subject, maybe the weather, the school, I don't know) and she starts tugging at the ankles of her hose. Then she moves up to tug at the knees. Then the thighs. Then she pulls up her skirt to her high thigh and goes up under her skirt and is pulling up there and doing the "adjusting the pantyhose dance" a bit. I thought that was a little ummmm.. unlady-like, but ignored it.

But then as she is still happily chatting away to me, she hikes her skirt up over her waist, which turns it inside out and now she can pull it up to her armpits and hold it there by closing her arms. With her skirt all up in her armpits, she grabs the waistband of her pantyhose and starts pulling them up to her bosoms (as old ladies say) as she starts doing deep knee bends to scooch them up. Ladies, we all know we've done this, but watching someone's Grandma do it in a public restroom is like walking in on your parents having sex, kinda' creepy. Mind you she's still chatting away while doing the deep knee bends and yanking her hose over her gigantic dark colored granny (literally) panties. I should win an award, I kept a straight face the whole time. My 13 year old daughter made believe she was fixing her sandals so her eyes didn't burn from the spectacle.

Grandma soon finishes up and wishes us well and exits. My daughter and I immediately turned to each other with the wide-eyed "what the hell was that?!" look and burst out laughing. After we get done in the bathroom and are walking back into the church, my daughter says "Oh Mom, that's so you in 25 years". And every time I told that story to my other 2 kids or my "Manfriend", they all responded with that same sentence! Hey! I know I'm a little quirky, and don't care what people think, and just make a joke out of everything but I'd like to think I had enough decorum not to yank my skirt over my head in a public restroom while I do calisthenics to adjust the crotch of my pantyhose!

Well, as I turn 47 this Monday, and my girls have had to stop me from walking into Wegmans with a giant ass-sweat stain on my khaki shorts (pleather seats and broken air conditioning in car do not a good combo make) on a scorching day... I guess only time will tell.

I Got Yer Turkey Right Here...

I'm sitting here waiting for my son to get off the train from New York City. This is the first time I've seen him since he left for college 3 months ago. I can't wait. However, I am trying to prepare myself for a young man who may be slightly indifferent and prefers to go see his friends. He's usually a loving kid but I remember how I was when I would come home from college... see ya' Mom and Dad!

I was thinking back on all the Thanksgivings of my youth. I was trying to think if anything unusual or humorous happened. I know it's totally unbelievable but in a family of six kids... there was never an "infamous" Thanksgiving. Not even any slightly humorous, unusual moments. Hmmm. perhaps I don't have the dysfunctional family that I imagined?

This year will be a little bittersweet, I'm happy my boy will be home, but it's the first year without my Dad. He passed away October 25th of this year (yea not even a month yet). While over the years I have had numerous Thanksgivings where he wasn't physically present since I live in New York State and my parents retired to Arizona 25 years ago, I spoke to him every year. I always speak to my parents every holiday if I'm not with them. I made a point to speak to my Dad on Thanksgiving because I knew it was his favorite holiday. My Dad loved to eat. It was almost a spiritual experience for him. And my Dad was not a fat guy, to the contrary my Dad was a runner all his life... which created the need for him to eat a lot.

I guess maybe that's the most notable thing I remember about Thanksgiving is my Father and Brothers running 10K races. I grew up 30 minutes south of Buffalo, NY. Every year my Father and Brothers went into Buffalo to run in the Turkey Trot 10K. Thank God nobody made me go and stand out in the freezing cold for hours to watch this race because they would have seen a tantrum of epic proportions. (And then I would have had my ass kicked and sent to sit in the car, so it's all good). Whoever else was home (there were six of us kids) stayed and "helped" my Mom. But the trouble was as we were being tortured with the saliva-inducing intoxicating aroma of cooking turkey, we had to wait for the guys to come home to eat. And wait. And wait. And wait.

My Dad and Bros always won their age categories, so of course they had to wait around for the awards ceremony. And it was downtown Buffalo and there were bars nearby, I think usually "having a beer" was involved afterward too. And back then there were no cell phones, we never knew when they were coming home. It was like freakin' waiting for Civil War soldiers to return home. Perhaps a carrier pigeon will arrive soon?

Then when they finally do walk in the door, they all had the nerve to want to take showers! Harumph! So what if you just ran 6.2 miles in freezing rain or snow and you are sweaty and wet and freezing... I'm hungry! Well, thank God we had two bathrooms each with a shower. Ok ok, you're clean, let's go. Oh no! My Mother, the Queen Mother as we have always called her, commands that all wet nasty running gear be hung on the clothesline in the basement or hung over the drainage tub. Jesus Mary and Joseph! Don't you people know what's at stake here?!!! Food! Food that's losing its freshness and warmth! I can only eat so many more cheese and crackers and relish tray items!!!

Finally, we can sit down! Yea yea "Bless us Oh Lord, and these thy gifts, which we are about to receive, from thy bounty, through Christ, Our Lord. Amen. " *Squeal* Oh my God, seriously we can't eat until everyone has filled their plate? What kind of proper by the Emily Post Etiquette Book family is this?

Ok, ok hurry up everybody, just get what you need, you can get more later.

Alright all done. Dig in! I'm so starved that I wolf it all down in 5 minutes and I feel like I'm going to be sick. Years later I learned the trick of pacing myself. In doing so, I would always be the last one sitting at the table with my Dad, who as I said earlier loved him some Thanksgiving. I would be slowly picking at my food as my Dad was piling on more helpings. I would try and talk to him but would have to wait until the chewing stopped just briefly enough for a quick answer. You know Emily Post and all...

I'm the youngest, so at various stages the older kids were drinking. When everyone was full of lots of wine and food and wanted to lay down in front of the TV and watch The Walton's Thanksgiving Special... My sister Jane and I insisted everyone come down to the basement to see the "show" we had been working on all day. Yea, I was that kid.

But karma is a bitch and I was subjected to many a "show" after holiday meals later by nieces and nephew and eventually my own children. As I begged in my head to please make it stop, I knew God was punishing me.

Oh look at the time! Time to go get the boy from the station!
 I had plenty of lovely Thanksgivings when my kids were young but they were a bit chaotic and I seemed to never sit down.
 Now as my kids are all teenagers I'm looking forward to some great dinners filled with laughter and love.

I'm Puttin' Your Ass on Hold...

Life has ups and downs, highs and lows, it ebbs and flows. Hey, I made a rhyme. Sorry, I'm a little tired, I'm easily amused. Those high points are sure great aren't they? Those low points can be soul crushing, can't they? But, guess what... silver lining alert! Those low points can be very educational and serve a great purpose.

I didn't think I had anything to write today as I am literally spent. I'm all out of mental gas. One daughter had oral surgery at the beginning of last week. Another daughter had major surgery to repair a deformed breastplate last Friday and she just got out of the hospital yesterday. Also on that Friday my son was going to a prom at another school. I spent most every spare moment when not working at the hospital and paid about $40 in parking for the week. And my son is graduating high school this weekend, and I had to attend brunches and ceremonies and whatnot somehow this week. My son goes to an all boys school, so they had a Mother/Son brunch and that damn thing made me sob like a baby as he presented me with flowers. Oy, I'm getting verklempt just thinking about it again. (and I'm not even Jewish) And I'm still trying to get the third one back and forth to school and homework done and finish up lacrosse season.

Ok, ok... so anyway. My point is not to say oh woe is me, and act like I have the worst problems in the world... I certainly don't. Just letting you know my mental capacity is diminished because of this load. Oh on top of all that, I had to empty out all my bank accounts to pay my sons $1,000 housing deposit for NYU this week. And I'm doing this all alone. Thanks, ex-husband, wherever you are. It's such a tragedy you are missing all your children's milestones. Oh, and I forgot to mention, I got a letter in the mail yesterday letting me know that after almost 12 years of legal divorce, my annulment was granted.

Makes one reflect and creates a certain sense of relief and failure.

Oh crap, see I didn't want this to be an unloading of my woes, but maybe that was a bit therapeutic writing that. Ok, so anyway, silver lining, yada yada... here it is. With all this stuff that was going on, I've had some other issues pop up, like some people needing attention or having problems they wanted to talk to me about or family members wanting to educate me on one thing or another, or even my own children bringing up things that just don't need to be handled right now. In the past I would have tried to handle everything, and put on my best crown of thorns and played martyr. But this time, (and it was kind of hard because I am a people pleaser) I just said no. I can only handle so much. I'm sorry if I hurt your feelings, please understand I don't dislike you, I'm just at capacity at the moment. No Vacancy.

Ya' know, when I was in college, I couldn't stand that God damn plastic doe-eyed Nancy Reagan and her patronizing and trite campaign of "Just Say No". As if complex drug addiction was that easy. Anyway, now I have some respect for her being 90 something and having lived with a spouse with Alzheimer's, that had to be heartbreaking. Anyway, I still don't like it but I adopted the "Just Say No" motto for some other things in my life. (I still think it's a dumbass anti-drug slogan though)

I had to firmly say, "I can't deal with this now, I will discuss it later". And if that didn't work, I just shut it down. I'm no good to my kids with an aneurysm or nervous breakdown in the hospital. And no one is going to put a damper on me enjoying my son's graduation either by causing drama. He's earned this, and so have I. I paid what wasn't covered by scholarships, I was there when he needed papers proof-read, I was there when that girl broke his heart, I nursed him through sports injuries, I drove him to every damn activity under the sun, I was there at fundraisers and plays and concerts and his sporting events, I took him on all the college visits. So bite me, you're not going to take this away from me. Cue James Brown... Say it loud, I'm a Grad Mom and I'm proud!

Going through tough times has taught me it's ok to say no. It made me realize when there were people in my life that suddenly shut me off (it was usually men that I dated that were going through a divorce), it wasn't personal (I hope), it was they had bigger fish to fry, and some chick they went out with a couple of times who started whining about why I can't see them was last on the list to deal with. Hey, it only took me 12 years to learn.

It was a two-fold learning experience, 1. It's ok to say no when you're overloaded. 2. Don't take it personally when someone says no to you. Saying "Thank you, I understand" and giving space will keep that a lasting relationship rather than pissing and moaning and trying to force someone to pay attention to you. Don't be so quick to judge, you never know what someone else has going on. It's not always about you or me; sometimes there are just bigger forces at work. Love and kisses, now leave me the hell alone!

2. RAISING CHILDREN

Whether you're a single parent or married parent, raising children is a monumental undertaking. I have been every kind of parent. I was a married parent, a divorced parent, and a single parent after my ex-husband disappeared and lost contact with us. Each has its own pros and cons. Married parent pro: There are two of you to share in the duties (allegedly). Married parent con: You may disagree on parenting issues and will be forced to sort that out. Divorced parent pro: You don't have to live with that scumbag anymore. Divorced parent con: When you have the children, you have them alone, no one to split duties with. Single parent pro: Everything is your decision, you don't have to consult anyone else if your kid wants to become an MMA fighter, you have sole say. Single parent con: Everything else… no money, no sharing duties.

But whatever type you are, I came up with a few items to consider in this chapter.

This Ain't 1979: The New Mom Code

I'm a one man band when it comes to raising kids. (I play a mean tuba and knee-cymbals!) I'm constantly running. My kids are slight overachievers and are involved in everything - sports, choir, band, theater, student government, friends. It's always something. And I support that because 1.) All that shiz got my son into a phenomenal school like NYU with scholarships. and 2.) None of my kids has even ever had detention let alone run-ins with the law or substance issues or promiscuity issues. Oh but wait, I know there's still time! The youngest one is only in 8th grade, keep your fingers crossed!

But me, my job history has been less than stellar and I've been broke trying to juggle being there for kids and work. I tried every trick in the book to have a job with flexibility but I didn't always choose wisely.

Having said all this EVERYBODY has something to say about it. Everyone wants to give me their two cents when I have a mini-meltdown about how tired I am of running around. I get everything from "only allow them one activity each" to "make them walk" to "make them wait at school while you work". To which I say - politely - fuck you and mind your own business, I'm just venting.

But it's when it comes to the special man in my life putting in his two cents, I can't really give him an FU if I want to keep things peaceful on the home front. I had to explain to him how things work these days as he has never been married and has no kids. And you know those people think they have all the answers.

Oh I can see how he has some valuable "outside looking in" advice but yea, it doesn't always work.

So I had to give a lesson on "The New Parent Code". Oh who am I kidding, we all know it's all about the Moms. "The New Mom Code".

First I had to tell him that it's a new world. It's not 1979 anymore where he was hitchhiking to his private high school and I was sitting at my high school for hours waiting for a ride after swim practice. Here's the difference...

In 1979 you could hitchike to school. In 2013 if you hitchike you end up on a milk carton.

In 1979 you could walk anywhere anytime. In 2013, I hate to be paranoid but there is a lot more risk. We live in a medium sized NY city and I have 2 teenage girls. If they are walking in a group, sure but alone, not so sure. Pervs and killers seem to be more abundant these days.

In 1979 if you were a latchkey kid you could go to school early and hang out and eat your Pop Tarts and listen to your transistor radio. In 2013 students aren't allowed in the school until 20 minutes before school begins. Probably to prevent all the free daycare they'd be providing.

In 1979 you could stay after school for a few hours waiting for a ride. In 2013 they would be calling Child Protective Services on your ass to see why you haven't picked up your kid. Not to mention you'd get a reputation with other parents (and students) as the parent that neglects their kids, which could be a fate worse than CPS.

In 1979 you could bum a sandwich or something off a lunch tray from another kid. In 2013 if you forgot your lunch, somebody's calling CPS again saying you don't feed your kid.

In 1979 you could show up at a neighbor kid's house and ask to hang out until your parent got home. In 2013 chances are nobody is home there because the parents are at work and the kid is at an activity because the parents work. Also if they were home, somebody would be calling CPS on your ass again saying you leave your kids home alone.

In 1979 you could send your kid to the corner store for smokes and beer. In 2013 a child can't even walk in a store alone without someone questioning them... and well the beer and smokes thing stopped a long time ago. Damnit. *snaps fingers*

In 1979 an adult could sit down and enjoy a meal while little Johnny went up to the bar to get them another Manhattan. In 2013 a child can't even be within like 10 feet of a bar or some such thing according to law. For Christ's sake how are they going to learn to be waiters as a second job to pay off their student loans some day?

In 1979 you could leave your kids home alone to go work the night shift. In 2013, you guessed it... CPS.

In 1979 nobody's parents ever went to any of their sporting events. In 2013 if you don't go your kid will cry because all the other parents go because everyone is a "helicopter parent" (a hoverer) and everyone judges you as the parent who never shows up to anything and obviously you don't care about your kid.

In 1979 18 kids could pack into a car with one other kid driving. No seat belts, no rules for teen drivers. In 2013, at least in NY State a kid can only have one family member in the car or no more than one other kid at age 16, then maybe 17 you can add one more kid. I don't know there are so many rules now. All I know is teens can't carpool to school or give each other rides home anymore.

You think I'm kidding right? No. It's a whole new world. My kid can't even wait at school or get a ride. I try to get my children rides with other parents but you definitely need to reciprocate at some point or they will stop giving your child rides as they are "the neglected kid that always needs a ride". And before you know it... yup, CPS.

It's funny how in this day and age most households have 2 parents that work. Living expenses require two incomes now with cable, internet, cell phones and high gas bills, things we didn't have in the past. And with a 50% divorce rate there are a lot more single parents households. Not to mention non-divorced single parents are very common these days when they weren't in 1979. However, society more than ever expects us to live like it's 1950 and all the Mom's stayed at home and could be available night and day. What gives, Beave?

Chill Out, it's Just Christmas Not a Death Penalty Trial

I've seen so many Facebook and Twitter posts lately that state how stressed out people are with the holidays. I was about to call the suicide prevention hotline for one woman, she seemed so on edge. I also saw another post that was so smug about how far ahead she was of the game with all her shopping and wrapping, I wanted to throw a shoe at her.

For the record, I would just like to state...

IT'S NOT A COMPETITION, PEOPLE! IT'S JUST CHRISTMAS!

Notice, I didn't say holidays? I just said Christmas. Ya' know why? Because I've never heard any of my Jewish friends stress out about Hanukkah! Ok, I've only heard one Jewish friend complain but it was mostly about having to get on a plane to see her older parents who like to eat the early bird at Howard Johnson's. Which, is usually just purely for comedic value anyway. However, she never complained about buying presents and decorating. Jewish folks make it simple, no tree, no decorations, one simple light fixture, eight days of presents so in case you forget something the first few nights... no pressure.

Kwanza, I admit I hardly know anything about and I don't know anyone personally who celebrates it. And most things I've read, those who do celebrate it usually celebrate Christmas too, it's not like it's an exclusive thing. I also believe it focuses on virtues and such, so again the principal is not about sweating stocking stuffers.

So, in the spirit of me being an adult survival guide, my advice to you is... chillax. What gets done, will get done. No one will notice that you forgot to put out your Wayne Newton dressed as Santa statuette. No one will notice that you only made a batch of sugar cookies and not peanut butter cookies. The kids won't care if you wrapped their stocking stuffers or not. Just try to enjoy the spirit of Christmas, family and friends. (yes, even if you hate your family)

And you might even say, "What about the kids? It's important for the kids." Guess what? The kids will get over it. I believe you might be teaching your kids a far more valuable lesson in life if they don't get everything they want this year. I kid you not, there were years my kids got construction paper or earrings or mittens from the Dollar Store. I cried and cried. Yes, I feel terrible that I can't give my children everything I want, but my children have learned that life isn't fair and to be thankful for what they do get. I'd like to think I won't be raising a bunch of spoiled ingrates. Oh believe me many times in my heart I wish I could raise spoiled ingrates just so they have nice things, but I realize the life lesson is ok too, and will last a lifetime, unlike an iPod.

Hey, didn't that Christmas angel say, "Peace on Earth, good will toward men"? THAT's what it's about! Please everyone, spread peace and good will to others, and accept peace yourself. That's really the key, peace within yourself, and it's uncanny how it spreads to others.

Take a deep breath and relish the simple joys. And remember, you will not be put to death by lethal injection if the silverware isn't polished or the stuffing is dry. Merry Christmas, Happy Hanukkah, Happy Festivus, Happy Kwanza to all and to all a good night! Peace!

Six (or so) Easy Steps to Taming Your Feral Child

In doing some research for my writing and its new direction, I came across a whole bunch of blogs on the internet written by Moms. However, most blogs are written by happy stay-at-home moms with small children and talk about crafts and their latest trip to Disney and poopy diapers. That ain't me. I'm past that phase. Now I'm worrying about my kids applying to colleges and staying away from kids who steal their parent's liquor. I'd worry about my kids stealing my own liquor, but I'm too broke to keep any around the house.

Oh, I know that poopy diaper world; I was there once, sans the Disney trips. You think you're the first one to ever have cute little kids and enjoy being a happy family, and you think we are all eager to hear about your kids... endlessly. Oh no offense to those moms, I've just been there, you want to share your joy. But I just wanted to say that sometimes in reading about all the cutsie wootsie stories you tell of all the adorable things that little McKenzie did... I think I would have booted the kid across the room.

And then the mommies even make jokes about being at their wits end with said adorable child. Oh honey, I feel like that every day, but it's not from having annoying kids it's from having busy kids. My children aren't perfect, I just figured out how to nip bad behaviour in the bud. I'll still get cranky kid attitude steered my way once in a while, but I don't get disrespect. Want to know how?

Well, I'll tell you how, because I'm nice like that. Parents... stay in control. Ain't no child ever paid attention to or respected a screaming, cussing parent. (Maybe they paid attention for the moment but it breeds resentment for a lifetime.) Did you when you were a kid? When my Mother went off, I just thought she was crazy, and as I got older... embarrassing. But when she just stopped and looked me in the eye, oh I had the fear of God in me. And the worst was when she was just quiet and told me I had disappointed her. OH! Stab stab stab!

Easy Steps for when your child talks back or has a tantrum:

1. Physically get down on eye to eye level with them.

2. Talk to them calmly, yet firmly, maintain direct eye contact. (you can't sound like Mr. Rogers, you must be firm and have a normal adult voice) If they look away, say "you need to look at me". State with authority that this behavior is not acceptable and we do not do that in this house. And keep it short, you lose them after about 15 seconds.

3. Ask them if they heard you and to repeat what you just said (or the gist of it).

4. Tell them when they can act in a civil manner, you will discuss it or continue with whatever the task at hand was.

5. Stand up and continue what you were doing. (unless there's blood to clean up or something)

If a problem is more involved you may need to discuss it with them. For instance, "Would you like it if I threw a Matchbox Car at you?" Or "Why would you deliberately take the paints out after I told you no?" Most of the time "No, because I said so" isn't the best answer. Kids need to learn logic and reason. Explain to them "We don't have enough time to paint, because we are having guests for dinner and I need to set the table".

Adults, do you feel better after someone explains why they said no, rather than just saying no? I rest my case. "Can I have a raise?" "No." My first thought is "I suck". But after they tell me they lost money in the 4th Quarter and just can't afford it, that I can accept.

And here's a tip for dealing with teenagers, instead of yelling at them when say maybe they didn't turn in their homework, flip the script and calmly ask them why they didn't do it? Not like an interrogation but more like "Do you not understand it?", "Do you have anxiety about it?", "Is your mind on something else?" You'd be amazed what kids start to talk about. Don't always assume your kid is "bad", there may be other factors at play and they appreciate you treating them like a human being. That won't excuse them they still need to have consequences but it will help them to not do it again.

I won't lie; it takes a great deal of patience on the parent's part. Oh and some kids may still flip out, it's not a cure all. But if you remain calm and CONSISTENT, I can almost guarantee you'll see the behavior improve over time. It needs to start as soon as they start talking though. Just laughing off bad behavior because they are "little" only creates monsters. (Have we not all learned anything from "Toddlers and Tiaras"?) It's never too early to start expecting respectable behavior from a child. Most important thing is, don't stoop to their level! Yea, I know we all have our limits, but even if you do have a flip out, apologize to the child and use it as a lesson that we all get stressed out, you know how the child feels. Keep the faith and have a cocktail after they go to bed.

How to Keep Your Daughter Off the Pole...

I've been in a relationship for the past three years, well only about a year and a half of it has been serious. That would be this last half of the relationship. Before that, I hadn't been in a serious, monogamous relationship since my marriage 9 years before that. (my husband didn't practice the monogamy part, but that's another story) Every time I make that statement that I was single for so long, people often ask me what the hell was wrong with me. I'd like to think that common sense was what was "wrong" with me. Well, maybe it was just guilt.

Oh I dated a ton during those 9 years. There were times I had two dates in one night. I had several instances of dating the same person casually several times over a few months but we never formed what I would call a serious relationship. I even let one man lead me around by the nose for years but I don't call that a relationship. I call that cruel on his part, incredibly stupid on my part. I'm not like some people who call a guy a boyfriend after two dates. I take relationships very seriously, I don't label anything as such until there is monogamy, expressing of feelings and coupledom (you know, planning things together).

There were men I wanted something more with but they didn't want it with me. There were men that wanted something more with me and I didn't want it with them. I was a Match.com fiend at some points, having conversations going with several men at once. It was fun, I wasn't misleading, we were all just trying to get enough information about the other to see if we wanted to meet in person. I could write a book about my Match experiences, oy. Maybe another time…

The point is I kept it all away from my kids, they didn't know. Why did I take this route in dating? Simple answer: because of my kids. No, I'm not some sort of saint, but it was just a natural first thought for me, "why do I want to subject the kids to my dating life?" When my ex left the house my children were 6, 3, and 18 months. I kind of thank God they were so young, because they didn't really notice much of a difference, their Dad travelled all the time with work, he was never home before the divorce. But still, I wanted them to feel as comfortable, happy, loved, and secure as possible. Also, within the year their Dad eventually moved in with the girl he cheated with whom the kids knew as an occasional babysitter for them previously. (oh yea, it's quite a story) So anyway, my thought was that was enough confusion for them, why add to it?

I only went out or went on dates when the kids were with their Dad on every Wednesday night and every other weekend. That part was really hard; I wanted to go out more, especially when I got asked out and had to say no, not tonight. No man ever came over when the kids were there; let alone sleeping over when the kids were there. Oh hell no! No man ever met my kids, unless it was by accident at the grocery store or an event or something.

The reason I'm telling you this is to show you it can be done, you can put your children first. Sure we all have been tempted to run away and be self-indulgent, especially after being hurt by divorce, but in the long run it's better for our most precious possessions, our children (and screw the PC, yes we do own them) to use some restraint in dating. If you don't, you will only be raising kids filled with resentment and abandonment and commitment issues, and then you'll be bitching later about, "I don't know what's wrong with my daughter working at the Klassy Kat!" Yes, you.

Also, if you keep moving mates in and out of your house, your children will also learn that relationships are not built on foundations of trust, love and friendship, but are slapped together out of convenience for temporary comfort, sex, and to share living expenses. And in return they will have revolving door relationships themselves all of their lives, I'm sure with multiple kids by multiple partners. Might as well have a deli counter take-a-number dispenser at your front door.

I've heard so many stories about women whose children didn't like their boyfriend, or men whose kids didn't like their girlfriend, and it was a bone of contention. Or I heard of people getting married and the kids hate the step-parent. Hey, guess what, maybe somebody should listen to those kids! It's not all about what the parent wants, you selfish bastards! Kids are pretty perceptive; they can spot a jerk before you do. And even if the person is very nice and you think the kid is acting out, you still need to address that. The kid is acting out for a reason, they have been through enough; they don't want to share you or have to deal with a new person in the house. Trust me when I say, you have to work through those issues first before you can plop somebody else into the middle of your family.

I won't lie, there were nights I cried myself to sleep because I was lonely and tired of going to every event at the kid's school alone. But today, as I look at my secure, well-adjusted kids, I thank God for keeping me on the path he did. (and I'm not overly religious) It wasn't always easy, but I feel good that I put them first. I knew men would always be there but my kids would only be young and impressionable once. And I'm happy that at least for now I don't think my daughters will be on the pole headlining at the Klassy Kat and my son won't be a multi baby-daddy. Knock wood, fingers crossed...

If You Don't Go to the Dance with Me, I'll Shoot You in the Face

Seriously, this is what it has come to. I'm afraid for my kids sometimes that (due to several incidences in the US in the last 15 years), if they look at a kid sideways, reject an invite to a dance, or laughs on 1st impulse when somebody trips, that that kid is going to go postal or stalk and beat a kid to death. Unfortunately, it's our new reality.

All right, since no one else is going to say it, I'll say it...

How the hell do you not know that your kid is on the verge of going mental and planning to shoot up his school? I say "his" because a girl has yet to go into a school with guns blazing, but ya' know; give it time I'm sure. So for the sake of saving pronouns, I'll just refer to the child as a boy. Ladies, don't feel left out...

I understand there are one or two kids that somebody did see the signs, they were taken to psychologists, undergoing treatment, yada, yada, and it still happened. I guess there is the rare case where a kid is just psychotic and when they snap, they snap. But I'm thinking, still, wouldn't he be under closer wraps, maybe taken out of the public school and put in a safer environment? Maybe store your guns away from the house?

Ok, psycho kids not withstanding... who the hell doesn't see this stuff coming? This kid in Ohio a couple of days ago, everyone said, "oh he was just a quiet average kid". The kid freakin' posted on Facebook he was gonna' shoot shit up! How much more warning do you need? Ok sure, kids talk a lot of crap. They exaggerate. But even if my kid were kidding about stuff like that, I'd be concerned and have a talk.

With several of these kids (what a shame I can use the word several in this sentence) involved in these school shootings, their background is... kinda' sad. To me anyway. They often live with Grandparents or Aunts or Uncles or whomever. Many times, not the parents. These kids are disposable kids to begin with. And I take it said guardian isn't paying that much attention. Those are really sad cases. What do you do? If Mom and Dad aren't deceased, then they should be taking care of their own damn kids! Yea, I know, my kid's Father abandoned them a couple years ago, and to me it's a crime worse than any except murder. There oughta' be a law. People need to stop walking away from kids, or don't have them to begin with! Step the hell up!

Ok, then you have the kids that did live with the parents like the Kleebold and Harris boys responsible for Columbine. Jesus, Mary, and Joseph! These two had arsenals in their homes and bomb factories in their garages and no one noticed? What kind of irresponsible parent are you?! They should be held responsible. I'm sorry; it's not that hard to keep tabs on your kids. I'm just flabbergasted on that one.

I'm not a perfect parent. But none of my kids has even ever had detention in their lives and I have 3 teenagers, one's about to graduate! (knock wood, let's keep the streak going!) But for the love of all that's holy, pay attention to your own God damn kid! Listen to them, talk to them, observe their moods, look at their Facebook and Twitter pages. You don't even have to be invasive by looking into their phone, just freakin' look at them!

I just... kids are my passion. They shouldn't be troubled, they should feel loved. Let's start loving them, paying attention to them, teaching them how to cope in the real world. When things don't go your way, marching into a place and shooting it up is not the answer. Communication and rational thought is the answer. Pay attention parents, that's an order.

In Defense of Television

I was watching a show that was introducing a segment about the Obama girls and what their life is like inside the White House.

I just saw the introduction, so I can't tell you anything in depth. Yea, I know, what a shitty investigative reporter I am… but it was like the Today Show or something and I had to leave for work. Plus Anne Curry was getting on my last nerve with her over exaggerated compassion face. So, I just saw the introduction…

Ok, ok get to the point… I have been so annoyed by what was said… I don't really know why, but… the introduction went something like this…

Scene: Camera 1 on Al Roker, cue Al…

"Coming up, we'll find out what the Obama girls do while they are at home in the White House, mind you, none of it involves anything you are doing now. The girls aren't allowed to watch TV, use the internet, computer, or use anything considered evil by the Amish" (ok I added the last part)

Are you fucking kidding me? The kids can't use any sort of electronics… oh wait, "during the week", he said… or have any connection to the outside world, apparently?

I just get so mad when people pull that "we don't watch TV" bullshit, like they are some sort of pompous elitist D-bags that think they are so above everyone else. Screw you! I love TV. And guess what, I even think it can make you a more well-rounded person. You watch the evening news, you are aware of important things going on in the world around you. You watch popular shows and you can have social conversations with co-workers, work associates, clients, potential mating specimens, etc. You watch documentaries, you learn shit. You watch sporting events, you witness history and witness some of the greatest emotional moments that human nature can provide. You watch HBO; you can learn where to find the best mother-daughter hooker teams in Nevada.

Ok, I didn't watch a whole lot of TV when I was younger, but that was mostly because there wasn't that much on, there were only 3 or 4 channels, and I was always at some sort of sports practice or doing homework. It was different in the 70s. But my parents still allowed us to be children, so we could relate to other children, and not be freakish outsiders, like the girl in my class who had college professors for parents who never allowed her to watch TV and just played Scrabble with them all the time and you felt like you were being interviewed by Dick Cavett when talking to her.

Now, there is so much information being thrown at us from every angle, every second of everyday, you become a sort of freak if you aren't aware of what's going on in the world and popular culture.

I had a very good adult friend who bragged about how she never watched TV or surfed the internet, and how she just read all the time. Good for you. But one day in the mid-2000s I said something about Al Gore and she said, "who?" Uh yea, you know the guy that used to be vice president? Um, that to me is embarrassing. But she was kind of proud of it. "Yea, I don't watch TV, so?" So? You sound kind of silly. And she was a businesswoman. I think you kind of need to know what's going on in the world to be a good business person.

Ok, it's one thing, if you just don't like TV. But at least just be aware of what's going on in the world, so you can have a conversation with someone and you don't sound like you live under a rock. I like TV. I enjoy TV. I take it at face value, it's entertainment. It's also educational. It's also informative. It makes me aware of important issues in the world. It makes me laugh. It makes me forget. It makes me see beauty in big gay drag queens, making their own gowns to perform for RuPaul… TV is good.

3. FINANCES

This subject is incredibly important. Not that "Children" wasn't, but often people don't realize the importance of financial planning. I don't even mean financial planning as in planning for retirement (although that is important); I'm talking about just having a budget... and sticking to it.

Some pieces were written about me, some about others. One essay was written after I had friends that kept stating how broke they were and how they were behind on their mortgage yet just got a new handbag or got their nails done or are going on vacation. This shit baffles me. Seriously. I guess maybe the thinking is, "I don't have enough for the mortgage payment anyway, so I'll just take what I do have and spend it on myself. Screw it." Uh, that's not how I work. That's just not common sense to me.

However, I have trained myself to just do without. It's really not important to me to buy "things" anymore. About twenty years ago I used to shop to fill a void, but now I concentrate on keeping a roof over my kid's heads and that pretty much takes care of the shopping urges. Thank God.

I Love Your New Prada Bag But Sorry to Hear You're Losing Your House.

Let me ask you a question... What's the first thing you do if you have financial problems? Is it?..

A. Go buy a new outfit because you're sad and that will cheer you up?

B. Go through your finances and see where you can cut back?

C. Open up another credit card because you need more cash flow?

D. Get hammered to drown your sorrows?

Go ahead, be honest. And I'll be honest with you, just out of college I would have chosen options A and D. When I was married in my late 20s, early 30s I would have chosen option B but my spouse would trump me and choose option C for us. And I have to admit, although A and D are still looking good,

I've learned that option B is the best. (damn you, common sense!)

I learned out of necessity and maturity of course. I've had times in my life where new expenses come into play (braces, new roof) or you're selling real estate and things are slow, your income goes down, your ex stops paying child support and I had no choice but to cut back. And yes, I even had to cut back on nightlife, ugh. But it's funny how people don't want to drink alone, you still go out with your friends and you say, "No, I'm not drinking, trying to save money", it almost becomes a personal mission then for them to get you drunk. Cheers!

I digress...

However, there were times when my income was cut in half, for instance after my ex suddenly stopped paying child support. It then becomes a situation of, you have for example $2,000 in monthly expenses and your income is now $1,000... at that point dropping HBO and saving $20 a month isn't gonna' do squat. Although, it's still a good idea to look at those things for the long run, the little things do add up, but at that point you need to make major changes like changing your living situation and getting government aid. Yes, folks that's a situation it's designed for, not a way of life, but a safety net for when you need short term help. But that is a whole other blog.

My point is... when the going gets rough, tighten up, don't go get your hair did and take a trip to Aruba. I know it may be a natural reaction (fight or flight, right?) to want to run away and indulge yourself and ignore it. (hey, haven't I mentioned that self-indulgent thing before? I see a pattern.) I can't tell you how many times I've been somewhere and someone is telling me all of their financial problems, like they are going to have to refinance their mortgage because they are two months behind, but in the same breath are telling me about their upcoming trip to Hilton Head. Uh, what's wrong with this picture? They may think they deserve it because of all their troubles, but it's just adding new ones... and it's making them look like an idiot.

There, I said it! Yes, I said it, other people judge you. Gasp! Normally that wouldn't really matter, but if you having to stop and think "What Would Other People Think?" will help you not do something stupid, like spending a fortune on something unnecessary, when you just blabbed about your financial troubles, then so be it. Stop spending money you don't have! It's really that simple. Keep a record of income and expenses, keep accurate track. Get rid of the credit cards, or keep them out of your wallet. Sorry, it might screw up the economy a little more but it will keep a roof over your head and save your sanity. You can do it!

Am I Supposed to Look Poor? Income Levels Should Have Uniforms.

I saw a status on Facebook the other day that said something to the effect, "If you're on welfare, how can you afford a smartphone?" Which made me think of this whole image problem I've had for a while.

My question is... if you're, shall we say... uh underprivileged, or uh living below the poverty line, or dare I say it "poor"... oh hell, if you're broke-ass broke... are you obliged to look the part?

Are you being a poser if you try to look "not poor" when you're poor? Or to think of it another way, if you are surviving with government assistance are you supposed to look the part? And what is the part? Dirty ratty clothes, a pair of brokedown Toughskin jeans, a pair of worn-out generic K-Mart sneakers, messy hair, and dirty finger nails? When you go to the Department of Social Services do you demand to see the "poor and huddled masses"? "Excuse me Miss, I'm here to inspect your dregs of society to make sure they are poor and huddled."

Here's why I bring this up. I know I'm like a broken record, but there was a time I was broke. Right now, I'm mid-range broke, but there was a time I was lowest of the low broke. Long story short, ex-husband split and stopped paying support, I lost my job, unemployment got held up for like 6 weeks, no savings, got evicted, yada yada. I had absolutely no income for 6 or 8 weeks with 3 kids. I entered hot mess land. I was cleaning friends toilets and writing real estate appraisal reports and ad copy for $10 or $20 here and there (I kid you not) for money to eat, while I looked for a full time gig. So, I went to social services, and that of course took a few weeks to get through the red tape, I think about 6 or 8 weeks later food stamps and heat assistance kicked in.

My background, grew up in a family with 2 parents who were Penn State grads, my Dad is a WWII veteran, both parents were white collar, we had belonged to a country club at one time, we travelled, eventually my parents owned a second home in Arizona, all six of us kids went to college, some advance degrees. I went to college in Maine for 4 years. Bottom line, basically I come from good stock and I'm educated, I ain't no slouch. Soooo...

When I had several trips to the DSS, I was thinking "how should I look?" Should I look like a Wal-Mart shopper? A dumpster diver? I remember judging people in the past and thinking, "you're in the welfare office, why are you wearing Baby Phat with your hair and nails all done talking on your smartphone?" We've all done it. Shut it! No! You know you have. I was still trying to work and going on interviews so I would be dressed and ready for work, coiffed hair and makeup. But I felt like I should go in there with no makeup, hair in ponytail, sweatpants, kids in just a diaper, smoking and yelling at my kids about kicking their asses.

My Catholic guilt is actually palpable, isn't it? You can see the visions of self-flagellation rising from my head, can't you?

My ex in-laws used to judge me all the time because I presented myself well, they thought I was taking the ~~mountain of~~ money that their son was giving me for child support and spending it all on myself. HA! My kids even defended me; they know I never spend anything on myself. They have to prod me to do it. I have gone a year at a time without buying a stitch of clothing for myself, only to be forced to because I wore out the crotch in my only good pair of pants or something. I am just frugal and have enough dignity to try and keep myself presentable.

My in-laws refused to believe that even though I looked fabulous, I was only wearing a 5 year old $79 coat from JC Penney, a $10 3 year old Calvin Klein sweater from Marshall's, a $15 6 year old tweed skirt from Marshall's, 5 year old $19 BCBG shoes from Marshall's. And I simply dried and straightened my own hair, tastefully put on makeup, and painted my own nails with a 2 year old bottle of OPI nail polish, and wore the only necklace and earrings I owned which were stylish pearls given to me by their son 15 years earlier. Is that so wrong?

By being properly dressed or wearing something with a label and having my nails done and checking my email on my smartphone that was a free upgrade at contract renewal time and is the only phone I have now, no home phone... I'm sure I have been labeled by strangers as a welfare fraud case a few times.

Some people think you should be "real" and look the part of whatever your income is. I felt bad for making myself look like a million bucks when I only had 59 cents to my name. It reminded me of that old Carol Burnett skit when she plays Scarlett O'Hara and her house had burned down but she comes to the door in a dress made from the curtains with the rod still in it. That's me... sans rod. I guess I'm more like the movie version. But I am kind of quirky, I would wear the rod. OK, nevermind.

I do have to admit that I feel really guilty when I go into Wegmans wearing fabulous heels and a dress, hair and nails done and I pay with food stamps. But again, did my own hair and nails, clothes and shoes were either from Target or Marshall's and a few years old.

I won't be on food stamps forever. I do work... a lot. But unfortunately for having 3 kids, my household size to income ratio is still below the poverty level. And I won't be as brazen as Old Dirty Bastard of the Wu Tang Clan and go on MTV and ride in a limo to get my welfare check. As I get higher paying and more frequent writing jobs, I'll be done with government assistance, but for now I need it. Now, had my ex paid his child support, I wouldn't need assistance. I didn't sign up to be a single parent, so I must keep plugging along to get to a level where I can provide as if I were 2 parents.

So, I just ask that the next time you see someone coming out of DSS or paying with food stamps at the store and they are well groomed and dressed properly... don't be so quick to judge. We all need help from time to time. Don't be hatin'...

Is a Sugar Daddy a "Want' or a "Need"?

Money is on my mind right now, a lot, so I share with you my brain bulimia. I've been binging on thoughts, now I'll purge.
 As I've said before, there have been times I've been destitute. Well, it's not only his fault; it's also mine that I don't have a degree in anything that would earn me any decent money. I work in marketing and a lot of times hours get cut, clients don't pay, times are slow, that's life. Everyone is quick to say, "Just find another job"... well yea because those $60k a year jobs are just falling out of the sky. *slaps forehead* Silly me, I forgot about that extra engineering degree I have, let's just go get a job in that! Not. Oh wait perhaps I'll just pull that nursing degree out of my ass...

So, times are tough for me right now. I need to find more project/job opportunities to make ends meet and feed 3 teenagers, which has prompted me to examine my budget.

This brings me to my first point, wants vs. needs. Y'all need to get this one straight. A "need" is something you must have to live, i.e. food, shelter, clothing. A "want" is, well... anything else. In lean times, paring things down to "needs" enables you to get by. Even when times aren't tough, trimming the fat and contributing more to savings helps prepare for future crises.
 Anyway, you need to be discerning about the needs, yes you need food, but surf and turf from Black and Blue is not wise when a can of Campbell's chicken noodle soup serves your dietary needs just fine. Not as pleasing to the palette of course, but it keeps you alive.

And you may be at wit's end and incredibly stressed out but a vacation is not a "need". Sorry. Neither is a new outfit, manicure, or cocktails. Oh no, not my cocktails! Uh, maybe we need to rethink that one. I'm Irish; booze to us is like oil to a car! Ok, ok just kidding. No, alcohol and entertainment are not a "need", much as we'd like them to be, they can be benched until we get on track again. *in fetal position sobbing*

Which brings me to my second point - the Sugar Daddy arrangement. I was discussing my issues with friends and someone of course suggested I find a Sugar Daddy. A Sugar Daddy is someone who lavishes money and gifts upon a woman just for the pleasure of her um, company. (Actually I have known kept women that said sex was not part of the arrangement) Now, me personally, I've never been able to take gifts, money, etc., from a man that I didn't intend to pay back or didn't have a deep, emotional ongoing relationship with and I gave back in love and support. I just can't use men. Sometimes I kick myself about that when I'm taking money out of my kid's piggy bank to buy some milk. But alas, it's either the Catholic guilt or honest upbringing that prevents me from taking some poor schmuck for a ride.

But sometimes I see these women that married for money, got divorced and are now financially secure to live on their terms... and I wonder if I'm stupid. It got me thinking, and someone told me there are actual websites to find these arrangements. Well, you know I just couldn't resist because people watching is like a drug to me. I'm like that kid who's Mom says to stay out of her room near Christmas time, and I'm headed straight in there, going in for the treasure hunt!

I went to a certain website and for experimentation purposes only, and signed up. Seriously, I didn't sign up to get a free meal, I just want to eavesdrop! I had to create a profile in order to browse others. As you all suspected, there aren't many "real" people on there, and those that are, are completely clueless of what a Sugar Daddy is and think they are on Match.com. Seriously, a few guys' profiles said, "I'm looking for a really sweet girl to love". Dude, really? Is the word "sucker" tattooed on your forehead? And some girls' profiles say, "I'm financially secure but I'm looking for a mature, sophisticated man to spend time with". Bitch, please. Either stop the denial, or go back to Match.

What have I figured out so far? Nothing. I'm determined to figure out if this Sugar Daddy (or Mama) thing is real and or lucrative. In the meantime, I'll be eatin' my damn soup... the side dish of integrity or stupidity is yet to be determined.

No One is Buying a Yacht with Government Assistance

As I'm sitting here getting a blown out tire fixed, I wanted to do something to pass the time. Why not write? What to write about?

Well, slap my ass and call me Sally, I found a draft I started ... why not finish that?

I'm a bit hesitant, as I'm not really in the mood to listen to some name calling from some anti-government assistance lunkheads. But I just want to share this story. And if I get hate mail throwing out the words, "liberal", "bleeding heart", "asshole", or other derogatory terms, I'm going to hunt you down and stab your tongue with a fork.

Here's my statement:

No one is getting rich off government assistance.

A lot of people bitch about people on government assistance. And yes, I'm sure somewhere there are people that try and cheat the system or are a little lazy and would rather collect some assistance than find a job. There are people who are not on the up and up everywhere.

In the same vain, there are incredibly rich people who cheat the system to not have to pay their fair share of their taxes. Is one better than the other?

But before you all jump to conclusions, let me tell you how it really is. I have at times had to seek public assistance. I'm a bit humiliated by it, but I had to do what I had to do, when suddenly left with 3 kids to raise alone with no income and no child support at a particular point in my life. I felt humiliated, defeated, depressed, and any other negative emotion you can name. Major FAIL for me.

And as I had to go through the process, I thought... who in the hell would go through this just to get some extra cash? You don't just walk up to a window and get money, and it certainly ain't no pile 'o cash. Let me break it down...

Have any of you ever been through the process? Until you have gone to a Department of Social Services office, witnessed the process, seen the people, I would think twice about spouting off about the "hoards" of people living the life of luxury off the government.

I've been through the process twice and on both occasions, it went like this:

1. Drive to one location. Walk in door, wait in line to go through security search and metal detector. Then go over to stand in line at info desk. when they get to you, tell your sordid story and they will give you the proper 18 page form to fill out and which line to go stand in next. Go sit down and fill out the 18 pages which includes very detailed financial and personal info (I was expecting a cavity search to follow). Go stand in another line for a good 15 minutes. When you get up to the window, tell them your sordid story again, they will assess your needs and decide which people you need to see. You are given a ticket with a number. You go sit down and wait... anywhere from 1-3 hours.

2. They finally call your number. You go into an office with a worker. Again you are asked to tell your sordid story. Your answers on the form are scrutinized. Who lives with you? What is your income? Are you legal? Closest relatives? Have you suffered from domestic violence? ...etc. they calculate facts and figures. Tell you what you might be eligible for. Then they give you an appt. which is days later at another location.

3. Days later... arrive at the other location for said "appointment" with all the documentation they have asked you for, Social Security

cards for all in household, tax forms, paystubs, copy of lease, child support docs, unemployment docs, photo ID, urine sample, and pap smear results. (not really on last two, but close) Wait in line, go through security, listen to some very large loud woman arguing about "Listen bitch, I ain't got nothin' in ma purse gonna' hurt nobody!". (true story) After you finally get through, you are told to stand in a specific line for a window. That wait in line is usually 30 minutes to 1 hour. You finally get up to the window to say you had an appt., they hand you a ticket and you go sit and wait 1-3 hours for the appointment you were supposed to have an hour ago.

The wait involves screaming babies and toddlers, Mothers yelling at said offspring, people yelling on cell phones, cranky people, bad body odor, too much perfume, and a metric ton of ass crack hanging out. Your number is finally called. You are yet again told to give your sordid story. You are judged, you are questioned, you are scrutinized, your documents pored over. They finally deem you worth or unworthy of different forms of assistance. You are then sent back to the original location to be photographed and finger printed and to receive your benefits card.

4. Oh it doesn't end there, there are several follow up visits (that involve the same wait time), workshops, and forms that come in the mail to deal with and must be dropped back down at office in person. Those 2 visits alone took up one entire day each, and were the most uncomfortable, uneasy thing I've ever had to go through. All the other document wrangling and protocol is quite time consuming and stressful as well.

And all of that to receive $300 in foodstamps per month for a family of four. I wasn't able to get cash or rental assistance, which maybe tops out at $400-$700 a month. For a family of four. Could you live off that? Do you still think people are living the "high life" off the government? Even with assistance you are still living below the poverty line. And in some instances they told me I made too much on unemployment to qualify, in others told I didn't qualify because I didn't have a job. Hello, that's why I need assistance!

Now, I accepted having to endure all that in order to get assistance. I desperately needed assistance. I am extremely grateful for the assistance; I couldn't have survived without it. I sucked up my pride and had to do what I had to do. But it just fries my ass when some of you think people would voluntarily go through that aggravating, time consuming, laborious process just for kicks! What's worse, the way they scrutinize your paperwork, and call and check with your employers and landlords, etc., I don't see that it's real easy to fudge your info.

Yes, yes I know maybe I'm naive, but I just don't think there is this vast conspiracy of millions getting rich off the government. An income of $800 a month does not make one rich.

However, I do agree that there may be some people who get used to the process and don't go out of their way to find a way out of the cycle of poverty. They are resigned to their lot in life. But the government does try to put programs in place to encourage people to get a leg up. However, when people start to bitch about let's cut the spending to these welfare agencies, the first to go are the people and programs that try to give the less fortunate a "hand up, not a hand out" as Sargent Shriver once said. It's a vicious cycle.

So next time you want to spout off about the "throngs" of people living off the government, think of what I just wrote. Just think first and get your facts straight. Just think, please.

Upside: Homeless Shelters are a Great Way to Make New Friends!

In today's chapter of Madge's Adult Survival Guide, we shall discuss...shelter.

I would say about... oh 75% of us have had trying times with our living situation at one point. No, not about needing a 3 car garage instead of a 2, or adding a home theatre. (bastards) I'm talking about things like...

- Divorce. Someone's gotta' move... where do you go?
- Job loss or other various money issues. Can't afford the mortgage or rent anymore. Where do you go?

- Dangerous living conditions. Abuse, bad neighborhood, crazy landlord, whatever. You know the question...

Sometimes it may just be a case of geography, "This place ain't workin', I need to go". That was my case living in Denver. I had moved there in 2000 when I was married, my ex had a job transfer. Then we got divorced and he eventually moved back East. I was there by myself, no family, some friends, but it just didn't really feel like home, and not to mention it was too damn expensive by myself! So in 2006, back East I went...

Was that a step backward? A step forward? Sideways? What? People often asked me why I moved to Rochester from Denver like I was some sort of intellectually challenged cretin. After a while I thought, "Hey bite me, I happen to like New York State! Ya' got a problem with that?"

I heard a friend mention taking a step backward in moving her kids and that prompted me to write this. Most all of us have had a time in our life where we need to regroup. For those of you that haven't and are still living in the same big house for 20 years... I hate you. Nah, you're incredibly lucky. Good for you. *grumble grumble* As for the rest of us, we've had to make tough decisions.

As I said, for the reasons above, some of us had to decide, (or had it thrust upon us) whether to move into an apartment or move home to our parents or friends or shelters or change locales. It happened to me, I got evicted from a house I was renting a few years ago here in Rochester. My ex-husband suddenly disappeared and stopped paying support, and my income was cut in half. I couldn't afford the house; I met with landlords and told them the circumstances, asked them to maybe find a new renter, etc. No, they decided they wanted to evict me and get all the money out of it they could. Really really unkind folks, especially since I was trying to negotiate this situation from the hospital, as I thought I was having a heart attack.

They would rather put a single mom and 3 kids out on the street, (because you know, "nothing personal", it's just business) than negotiate a fair deal for legitimate reasons. Anyway, decisions had to be made, and I believe in karma...

Various family members have wanted me to move in with them. I love love love them for the offer. But that meant yet another move to another state. With kids in junior and senior high school, I just wasn't going to uproot them again. I just knew in my heart it would not be good in the long run.

So I borrowed money for a security deposit (since the eviction cost me several thousand dollars that I didn't have) and moved into a townhouse style apartment. Living in an apartment complex blows after I've lived in some nice houses with yards. But what am I gonna' do? I did what I had to do. Biggest casualty... my pride. I used to love to entertain in my house, now I don't want people to know where I live. We used to be the hangout house for kids, now I'm embarrassed to have kids over. Oh well.

So, that's the dilemma... is it a step down? Yea, going from a house to an apartment is probably looked upon as a downgrade more than an upgrade. It sucks. I sure didn't feel like singing The Jeffersons theme "Well, we're movin' on up!" I live around some less desirable people than I'd like. There are two bedrooms for four people; my son doesn't even have his own room. The place is small, the kitchen is 5x5, and so is the one bathroom for me and 3 kids. I don't have a garage. I can't paint or redecorate or plant things. The kids don't like the trashy people that roam the parking lot or hearing the neighbors through the walls. But... I can afford it. And we stayed in the school district, and because of it my son will be going to one of the best colleges in the country next year. I'd like to think I won't be there forever either. I have plans, hopes, dreams. That's all I can do.

You just have to do what you can do. What's best for you and your children, spouse, parents, whatever the case may be. The most important thing is to really think it through and put your pride aside. Sometimes you may have to think of the short term, other times think it through to the long term. Make a list of options, pros and cons. And for the love of God, DO NOT move into someone you're dating's place if you have kids, just because it's convenient or you don't like to sleep alone! Eh, maybe if it's for a month or two, while you're in transition from one place to another or something, but Jesus, Mary, and Joseph, don't make relationship decisions based on saving on your cable bill or loneliness! Seriously, please, just say no. Think it through. You may not have the best home, but you can take pride in knowing you are doing the best thing possible for you and your family.

4. RELATIONSHIPS

The following post is why I did not include any of my earlier writings in this collection. Although they may have been funny, they were embarrassing. Well they would probably be entertaining to you, ya' know like watching a car wreck of a seriously misguided and hurt woman... I just feel stupid about them. Which is also ironic for me because I thought I knew it all.

I was just packing up my house to move and was looking through some boxes that hadn't been touched since my last move. I found about twenty self-help books that I bought or was given right after my divorce. I guess it's part of my anxiety and ADD, I have no patience I wanted all the answers and all the healing done immediately. Some of it was good advice, but most of it I just dwelled on way too much. I was just going to have to go through what I had to go through and that was that.

It wasn't pleasant but I got through it. I finally got to a place where I didn't feel hurt, angry, and lonely all the time. I would be perfectly fine being all alone right now. And I sincerely mean that and that is a first for me. It's not right or wrong, it's just where I feel peaceful right now… and that is all that matters.

How to Lose a Guy in… Ten Minutes.

As I try to figure out a new direction to take my writing in, it occurred to me, why not write about all of the stuff I couldn't write about before? The stuff I'm talking about is all of my dating adventures over the past 10 years while I was divorced and dating, ya' know pre-relationship. I couldn't really tell all, since some of the people involved were reading my stuff, and that would have been awkward. However, the twist is, it won't all be making fun of all the psych ward escapees I encountered, it will be a lot of revelations of things that I did wrong.

Oh yes, Madge was wrong. Hey, I admit it. A lot of you that read my writing back in the day will probably say "We coulda' told ya' you were wrong!" Yea, yea ok, sometimes it takes some of us a while. Sometimes people never learn. I'd rather be wrong and have figured it out than still be convinced I'm right and still be alone and miserable. Once I became generally unmiserable, my whole life, not just dating changed. I got back on a career track, and the kids and I started to thrive.

Wait, let me clarify, I wasn't miserable because I was alone; I was just miserable, period. Now, I could be alone and be happy. Make sense? Moving right along...

I used to think I knew it all. I was convinced that brow beating a man into honesty and forcing his hand was somehow a sure-fire way to attract them to my womanly wiles and fall madly in love with me.

Bah hahahahahaha!!!!

I was so obsessed with honesty after my lie-filled marriage that I became "Date-zilla". It was all about laying all the cards out at once, and if a man followed-up on our date I would go into interrogation mode about his intentions. And if they weren't what I wanted, I pouted, and was passive-aggressive, and did the guilt thing. Oh, I was convinced that I didn't do that... but I did. At some point I think we should all be videotaped in our lives, because sometimes what we perceive we do, and what others see are two vastly different things.

Oy, I hate to admit it, but it's true. Of course, it wasn't with everyone, a good number of guys I was trying to ditch because I just wasn't attracted. I would say 90% of the men I met just weren't interesting to me. I was very picky. But there were ones that could have had a chance, had I not blown it. However, I do think things happen for a reason.

Once I started to learn to be confident, act like I didn't care, and set up boundaries and walk away when the boundaries didn't suit me... things started to go my way. That was the tough one, walking away after the boundaries were set.

Sometimes you want something so bad, you make a bad decision and say, ok screw it I'll go meet him just this once. As they used to say on Family Feud, "X". Wrong answer. The fact is the guy I'm dating now, my boyfriend (oh that word still seems so silly at my age), didn't start really respecting me until I said no to the nonsensical situation he wanted to have with me. I thought I was being cool saying I was ok with a casual dating thing, but yet being passive-aggressive to him about wanting a relationship and then really being hurt when he went out with someone else.

Truth be told, I wanted a relationship with him and it was ok to admit it and walk away if he didn't. I was raised by a pack of angry feminists to believe relationships weren't important (yet the twist was, once you were in it, it was for life). Yet I finally was shown that it's ok to want love, especially after 10+ years without it. It's not ok to be addicted to it and be a Liz Taylor. But I had to accept it was ok to want love, and stop fighting it internally. That was a lot of what made me angry inside.
   However once I accepted it, I needed to keep my standards and boundaries and hold out for the right relationship. I had to learn patience, which is not an easy task for me... it was like teaching Sid Vicious to "just say no" to heroin. But as Dub-ya once said "Mission Accomplished".

Is Your Relationship MIA, POW, or DOA?

When do you call it quits in a relationship?

Call it... time of death on this relationship, 3:42pm.

I've been thinking about this because during the past year, I've been going through the process of an annulment. I've been divorced for 11 years, but I've been thinking about the future and what if I want to get married in the church again. Or who knows maybe the annulment is my way of getting in the last word with my ex since he disappeared, with a final F-U from the church?

It's a very intense, invasive process. You have to tell your story over and over and over again. Relive all the pain. All to see if your relationship was non-existent, no connection, too volatile or one sided. Then they make you have witnesses who have to write up their stories on your relationship and hand them in. Now they're trying to extort more money from me by saying they need a professional psychological evaluation of the situation. Really, how much more proof do you need than 5 people's testimony that the husband was a raging alcoholic and bi-polar? Oy.

Now don't get all "organized religion is bad" on me. That's not the point here. My point is, in replaying everything I think there were times I should have left early on before any more kids were born, but then I wouldn't have had these fabulous babies I have. So, no sense in rehashing that. But then I think should I have stayed longer? No, I think I got out just in time, I think things were going to escalate into serious domestic violence on his part. I was a prisoner not a wife. Is there ever a right time to end a relationship? I think more often than not, people over stay their welcome, just to make sure it's really not going to work.

It's like going to a shoe store, you fall in love with a pair of shoes, you try them on but they don't fit. So you try them on again. Still don't fit. Go look around in the dress section, come back, shoes still don't fit. Go look at purses, come back, try to ease your foot in ever so gently tenderly lovingly... shoes still don't fit.

Get my drift? Should you have bagged it after first try? Maybe, but you do love those shoes. After the second try? Probably. Are you wasting valuable time in persistently going back to those shoes, when you could be moving on to other purchases? Maybe. Only you know... and the Catholic Church apparently. Obviously they are the only other people to know when and how a marriage should be declared ripe for never having existed. I really hope they don't read this, my annulment will be screwed. Oh well, I think I know that I made the right decision at the right time for me. What good does it do to second guess? Maybe it could? I don't know...

In Love There are No Victims, Just Volunteers

I used to be the one that had all the answers.

That was part of my huge problem with men in my 8 years of post divorceness.

I was so busy trying not to get fooled again, and trying to be right rather than happy... I just fucked it all up.

I read a an article recently of someone who is dating again after being in a relationship for a while. There have been all sorts of misadventures. I was the same way. I wanted to know why every man didn't call, or said he liked me, or stood me up, or why he wouldn't sleep with me, or why he did want to right away... I had to analyze everything.

The most valuable thing I found out in the last 6 months has been...

Sometimes shit just happens and you just need to leave it alone.

If a guy didn't call... he didn't call. The reason doesn't matter because there's nothing you can do about it. Ignore it. Move on. If you really felt something may have happened or there was a miscommunication, you can give one more very brief try in the form of one sentence, "Sorry we missed each other, I'd still like to get together if you would?" And that's it. No interrogation. No analyzation. No speeches. No telling them, "I know you didn't call me because you are one of those guys that just hold out until the best offer comes in..." Just let it go. Move on.

That was something that took me years and years to learn, that I don't have to interrogate everyone. Perhaps in a past life I was part of the Spanish Inquisition. I was convinced no one was going to pull one over on me, and I would tell them so, and in doing that, I lost the last thread of a chance I probably had, (if I still had one) since the reason why they didn't call was because their ex got drunk and they had to unexpectedly take the children but didn't want to have to tell me that. Or perhaps, they just weren't really feelin' it with me. I finally figured it out that it's not a crime against humanity to not be attracted to Madge. *Gasp!!!* Hey, I figure I'm only attracted to about 1 out of every 20 guys that's attracted to me over time... people just aren't interested in dating everyone they meet.

I was playing the victim. Poor me. What a pain in the ass I was. Yea, there are times you want to vent and you exaggerate, "The world hates me!!" Eh, it's ok to let those out every now and then, but I know I went through a period of a few years where I really thought that.

I got over that.

I was listening to a great radio interview today with an author who wrote a book on sexual betrayal. She was awesome. She was saying, and I COMPLETELY agree that almost every time (there are always bizarre exceptions to everything) that a person cheats it has nothing to do with their partner, it has everything to do with the person that is doing the cheating. When people cheat, they are doing it to fill a void in themselves or to get a quick high or some other thrill. That's exactly what my ex did. I know that he has serious problems and nothing in this world will make him happy until he fixes himself on the inside and makes himself happy.

There was a guy on internet circles that swore up and down that he cheated or attempted to because his wife cut him off from sex. I don't know the whole story, there are always 2 sides, but it seemed to me that person was a little needy anyway. Sure not having sex can drive one to find it in other ways if the need is that strong, but I would think you would seek help first and if it's really bad have the courage to walk away first. Some people just want sex for attention. My ex-husband treated me like shit and I never once cheated. Didn't have it in me, I had enough strength and self-esteem to know that I shouldn't do that.

What's my point? The point is, nobody owes you a thing. Nobody has to like you. And if they cheat on you, don't play the victim, have enough strength to know that they are just douchecopters and you are above that. Being a victim and getting revenge only makes you look like an ass. Don't go vandalizing his stuff... you don't look strong, you look like a psycho. The best revenge is to just dump his ass and move on. Well, and it doesn't hurt to tip the police that he sells weed, either. Just kidding! But either way, you're better off without him/her. Good riddance to bad rubbish...

My Date With a Serial Killer

It's probably not a wise idea to determine that you want to go forward with something just because you don't want to do the alternative ever again. Like deciding to quit high school because you never want to take a test again. That's stupid in the long run, know what I mean? Besides, you'll be "tested" all your life, dumbass. Pull up your skirt, Sally and get back to work.

So should someone decide to get married just because they never want to date again? I've actually heard that decision announced before. Now having been married and withstood a long period of dating post-divorce, I'm tempted to go hide in the confines of marriage after what I've encountered.

What got me thinking was going out for my birthday this week to a restaurant that's hot with the middle age single crowd. I soon noticed it was all the exact same ~~lame-os~~ people that were there three years ago the last time I was single. Then I started to stroll down memory lane, taking inventory of all my dating exploits as an adult. I'm surprised none of my dates have shown up on America's Most Wanted as a psychotic serial killer. I can think of one in particular...

It was probably 8, 9, 10 years ago (I forget, I've blocked it out) I was living in Denver and regularly doing the Match.com thing. This isn't an "all people online are crazy" thing, I met a few rather nice fellows, this one just happened to be a shit show. I started exchanging emails with a decent looking, charming, stylish gentleman a few years older than me. Now, once I start to tell you his details you will probably think,

"Madge how could you possibly believe this asshat?!" Now mind you details were leaked slowly as if he were a punctured natural gas line.

Some details escape me like if he had been married or had kids, but I do remember he said he didn't live around Denver, he only visited occasionally for business. Then there was something about owning a vineyard somewhere and had a wine label. Now that is not entirely impossible as there are thousands of small wineries in this country. Eventually he tells me he was orphaned as a child as both of his parents died in a car accident when he was a baby. It could happen. Then something about being taken in by an Italian couple... I'm also remembering something about sending a baby up a river in a basket with a Hebrew slave cloth, but I might just be confused, it was a while ago. Oh no that was a movie (and the Bible). He said he spoke Italian but I soon realized he only ever seemed to throw out the same 4 or 5 Italian words.

The lies got more elaborate, as the couple turned into wealthy Italians who lived part-time in Europe and he had or would be inheriting all this stuff. Anyway, the more suspicious lies were coming out after I agreed to meet. I think I just met him in person just to see what would happen with the stories.

So we meet at a local hotspot. He walks up to me and he looks somewhat like his pics but you could tell they were from several years earlier.

He wasn't terrible looking and he had some expensive-looking European clothes. So we sit down and he orders a Maker's Mark for himself and me a Bombay Sapphire and tonic. He keeps stressing how he's not from around these parts. He slams his drink and quickly orders another one for himself and me. Um, I had barely taken a sip of the first one you ordered me.

As conversation goes on, I start to question his stories. It seems I'm calling him out a little. He appears a little agitated and takes me out on the dance floor. As we are out amongst the crowd, all these folks keep saying hi to him and giving big hugs and kisses. Um, thought you didn't know anyone? He said he met them on his trips here. Then I'm starting to eavesdrop, because every time a person would come by he would turn away to have a conversation. This is when I started to hear things like "Have you found a job yet?", "Everybody back where you work at blah blah down the street misses you", "Hey, how's your brother?". I was furious, yet humiliated I fell for it. However, I didn't really "fall" for anything, I kinda' knew, but it was like a car wreck, I wanted to go look to see if there were any survivors.

We go back to the table he immediately orders another drink, as I have two unfinished. When the drink came, I said, "We'll have the check", because I knew the "date" would be ending after I said my peace. I had a big smile and said, "Ya' know I heard all of your conversations, I know everything you told me was a lie". I didn't even get mad; I tried to let him off the hook. But do you know what the m*****f***er does? He starts yelling at me about.. what, I don't remember because I was busy picking my jaw off the floor. Something about me being a bitch and negative and thinking I'm too good... then he slams his drink down his throat, throws the bill at me and stomps out.

Yes, scumbag leaves me with a 40 something dollar check and a bag of bullsh*t. I was so mad about him inhaling drinks and stiffing me. No not that, I meant sticking me with the bill. But I could do nothing but laugh and shake my head and wonder what he was thinking. Maybe he was so depressed about his life he wanted to pretend to be someone else for a while. That seems to happen a lot on the interwebz. How long did he think he could ride these stories? It's like people showing up to a date 100 lbs. heavier than their online pics, do they think you'd be blinded by their stellar charm and ignore it? But I take responsibility for getting duped, well not duped because I was skeptical to begin with. Let's just say curious. However for the future, I don't recommend going out with someone if you think they're lying, it could be dangerous. Obviously he had a temper, it could have ended worse.

But should I take a dive into the security of marriage just because I don't want to deal with the prospect of that happening again? Probably not a wise idea. Yea, lots of widows back in the day used to just marry a guy to get health insurance again even though she knew he beat her kids. Eh, what are ya' gonna' do? What you should do is weigh all sides equally, good and bad and make a sound decision. And have the balls to face stuff you don't really want, don't go hide under your security blanket as an alternative. You're gonna' have a few thorns amongst the roses.

When Unrequited Love Becomes Requited Crap

Everyone has some unrequited love goin' on. Oh, balogna (that's such a dumb word, it should be baloni or baloney, but I guess it's like how capacola became "gobbagool", anyway...), you all have that one person you say, "what if?" about.

Oh yea, the levels of intensity of the "love" vary. It can be anything from the kid that used to mow your parents lawn that you never said two words to or it could be someone you dated a bit and the relationship got cut short for whatever reason. It could be you thought your lover drank the poison but they were only sleeping, so you killed yourself. Oh wait, you wouldn't be reading this then...

I've had many of these in my life. Hey, I had a lot of crushes as a little girl, I'm not a ho. There were a few boys from high school that I would have liked to date but couldn't because I had a steady boyfriend. So, there's that. Then I had the steady boyfriend that fizzled out when he went to college and I moved away. In the early 80s there weren't cell phones, or Skype, or IMing to keep you together. But I'm always curious to know how that relationship would have played out in our adult lives.

To requite or not to requite, that is the question! I'm here to tell you... I've requited. Yes, yes it's true. Thanks to the internet, after my divorce I got down to brass tacks, went back to basics, put the cart before the horse... wait what? Uh whatever, I ran across some blasts from the past.

There was the internet thing but a couple of times it revolved around high school reunions. I'm telling you folks, you need to go to these things. It's excellent for networking and dating. So you had a bad time in high school? Get over it, walk in with your head held high, and use those people for getting ahead in your world now! Anyway, one of my run-ins was with a boy who was my "boyfriend" in 5th grade. I broke up with him because he tried to give me a Minnie Mouse ring, and I knew if I came home with it my parents would ask where it came from, then they would know I had a "boyfriend", I would get an hour long lecture/screaming at and my 11 year old self would never be let out of the house again until I was sent to the convent.

Fast forward, I ran into that "boy" later in life and we eventually got together and had an amazingly awesome time. But... it didn't get into a serious thing because we were geographically several states apart, I just got divorced, still had little kids, and he was still a raging never been married playboy. I took it at face value, I'm glad it happened. And now he's married and kicking himself.

However I had a couple others (Stop calling me a whore! These have taken place over 12 years!), that it, well it just was less than stellar. That kiss you had waited 30 years for was like... "oh, that's it, that's what I waited for?". Or that happy go lucky boy you had the crush on is now a neurotic mess and is starting to stalk you. Um, yea. I won't go into specifics but it just wasn't good, but overall I'm glad it happened. Now I know. I still have the fond memories of the younger crush but don't have the pangs of want. Know what I mean?

Those were kind of fun but the ones that are more intense are the unrequited adult loves. Oh, they can be so difficult... Or not. A difficult one was deciding to move back East when something was never totally finished out West. The "or nots" can be disappointing or funny. I remember running into a guy years later after I had gone on a date with him post divorce. I thought he looked great. We went out again in those later years and... I remembered exactly why I didn't want to go out with him again years before. He was nice but very self-impressed with the personality of a bag of wet hair. Another guy I had gone out with, we never got intimate but had obvious sexual chemistry. Years later we got intimate and it was what I imagine sex with a quadrapalegic with Tourette's Syndrome would be like. Yes, that bad. *heavy sigh*

But I had some others I haven't revisited and still wonder what if? What if we both hadn't just been divorced and both been messes? What if we didn't always run into each other when we were dating someone else? What if your previous girlfriend hadn't found out she was pregnant by you? (yea that happened)

I don't know. I do like knowing the ending to the story. I'm not a big fan of not knowing. It's my anxiety. I never could go to sleep on Christmas Eve. Others will say not knowing is part of the fun, the fantasy. That's why some people you meet online play games with you, they have no intention of meeting, they just like the fantasy of the hunt. Yes, those people really exist. Not me, unless you've given me giant red flags, I just have to know how the story is going to end. And unfortunately that one did not end well. Oh well, next...

5. JOB/NO JOB

Oh Lawd, on this section, girl I could write a book. Well, I kinda' did, but this is just a chapter. Perhaps that will be my next book

I don't know how I have had so many jobs in my life. I'm still trying to figure it out. Oh who am I kidding, it's because I pick the wrong jobs, they bore me, I have a short attention span and I want to do too many different things. And I hate people. I love people from afar and socially, but really I hate working with people the older I get.

As you'll find out in the next chapter, I've had a hard time making ends meet over the years. Next chapter? (Nevermind I know I said it about ten times in previous chapters). Several times I was thrown into bad situations, had to somehow suddenly support everyone (or just myself) and I usually panicked and picked the first shady job on Craigslist and ended up being let go as the business was folding. Then I was always listening to everyone else about get rich quick jobs I should try... real estate, sales, home party products, work from home. It was all a bunch of crap. Well except real estate, unfortunately the housing bust happened in 2006 and ended that for me.

Here is a collection of essays I wrote about finding a job, a career, your niche in the world. They were usually written during one of my countless job searches as I tried to sort it all out.

Hire Me, I Give Good Hair!

Having been born a creative being is a blessing and a curse. Oh, I have a lovely imagination and can be mildly entertaining, but financially... I ain't gonna' lie honey, it blows. Blows like a humpback whale.

I went to college for four years in the mid-80s for broadcasting. It was a new up and coming "thing". But it turns out when I got into the field, no one else had a degree in broadcasting, you didn't need one. Any schlub could get into radio; in TV you needed to at least have good hair. Oh the industry paid minimum wage, they didn't have to pay more because everyone was clamouring to get into radio and TV because they thought it was so cool. It was kind of cool, but it was also run by major league nerds-turned-narcissists. The worst kind.

The industry then got even more competitive as ownership rules loosened and stations were consolidating. I needed to reinvent myself. The route I chose at the time was stay at home mom but I still did some marketing stuff on the side that I learned while being a sales assistant in TV. Thus began my long journey of doing piecemeal marketing work and searching for jobs on and off for 20 years.

So, I feel well-qualified on the topic of job searches. I may not always find my dream job, but I guarantee you, I always find a job. Something, anything. I don't understand when someone says, "I've been out of work for a year". I do understand that sometimes you can make more on unemployment than working retail or some other entry level job, but if it's been that long, it's time to regroup. And you have to accept the fact that you will probably have to take a job that's barely tolerable until you find your ideal job again. Life isn't fair, stuff happens, pick up your purse, Sally and suck it up.

In this economy in the past few years, job loss is all too common. Everyone knows at least one person, if not many, who have been affected. Once again I find myself looking for a job after having my hours cut at my current place of employment. Unfortunately in my line of work, (marketing) my job is always the first to be cut when things are slow. I would love to make writing my full time job. Anyone want to hire me?

Ya' see what I did up there? Anyone? Bueller? Bueller? I asked for help. Rule number one; let everyone know you are looking. Don't beg and whine or make a cardboard sign and stand on the corner of Monroe Ave. and I-490. Be dignified and matter of fact. A simple Tweet or Facebook status, even a broadcast email to friends... "I'm currently looking for a position in Prehistoric Pancake Making. If you or anyone you know hears of any openings, I would greatly appreciate it if you could let me know. I'll be glad to help you in any way I can, as well. Thanks." It's as easy as that. You'd be surprised how many people love to help. The key to finding a job really is in "who you know".

Rule number two... Network, network, network. Oh and did I say network? This is a supplement to letting people know you are available. Get out and meet more people and let them know you are available. I know it may be tough for the less sociables out there, but it really has to be done. There are so many networking events in my town, it's ridiculous. Yes, they are mostly all free, sometimes there is maybe a $5 fee, but there are plenty to be had. Get online and look up "networking events". Also LinkedIn has tons of groups promoting networking events. Also your local paper (available online) usually has a calendar of events. If you are really stumped, just email me, I'll direct you on where to look.

I could go on and on with tips, but that's a good start. Jesus, I can't hold your hand! You gotta' just jump in and get going! Well, but wait, you do need a decent resume. Have someone

dependable look yours over before you start sending it out.
And if you really suck at resumes, I HIGHLY suggest having a professional do it. I write for a living and I still had a professional look over mine. Hey, even bestselling authors have editors; another pair of eyes is always wise. Take it from your Auntie Madge. Oh good Lord, I started channelling "Hee Haw", it's time for me to wrap it up...

It's all in who you know. Start talking. Ask for help. Circulate resumes. Get on LinkedIn. Be unique. Stand out. Hire Madge for all your marketing and writing needs. *wink wink nudge nudge*

Networking: When Awkward People Attack!

Yesterday I went to a networking event. I really have to be in the right mood to attend those things. Sometimes I feel sociable, other times, not so much. I used to feel sociable all the time but in the last couple of years I feel like just sitting in the corner with my dirty martini and waving off anyone who dare try approach me.

Networking events, parties, hanging in a bar, it's all sort of the same thing. Some people are natural socializers, others are not. I'm great with other socializers but over the years I've gotten increasingly more irritated with the socially awkward folk. You know the kind... they don't say much but stand there and laugh nervously, yet they still follow you around, staring at you with nothing to say. Or the folks that, trying to get them to elaborate is like trying to get Kim Kardashian to wear less eyeshadow. They only give you one word answers and then just kind of stand there with a half-grin on their face.

I'm usually quite awesome at reading body language and social cues. If someone starts looking around, or seems bored talking to me, I walk away (ya' know, politely of course). Hey, I can't always be the most captivating person in the room, I let others have a chance. I'm a giver like that. I can also tell if I have offended someone, I change the subject. I can't help it if everyone doesn't respond well to my stories of expressing my dog's anal glands. (just kidding, I don't have a dog anymore, nor would I discuss that with strangers). Let's face it, I am the picture of Emily Post when it comes to party etiquette. Too bad not everyone else is.

Other social types I can't stand:

The Close Talker - get the f*ck out of my personal space, for Christ's sake! And take a shot of minty Scope while you're at it.

The Lecher - The guy who has some close talker tendencies who is staring down your blouse the entire time and is always trying to turn the subject down the naughty road. (he's not getting anywhere near my naughty road) Or maybe he thinks he somehow has magical bedroom eyes and is trying to put you under his spell, staring you directly in the eyes with a come hither look. Um... that's just creepy.

The Cling-On - This is the female version of The Lecher. I've been out with guy friends and seen this happen. Again, she has close talker tendencies and amazing posture. Somehow her breasts always end up brushing against you. She's usually sloppy hammered and can't take a hint that the guy is not interested even if she put a bag over her head and had a car waiting for her afterwards.

The Puppy Dog - The lone guest at his/her own pity party. They start off the conversation by telling you their Mother died and they are unemployed. Much like Debbie Downer but with the addition of following you around waiting for a crumb. What? What do you want me to do?! I don't know whether they want money or pity sex, but the approach ain't workin'.

The Peddler - At networking events they could really give a crap what anybody else has to say, they are not there to learn about what anybody else does. They come armed with fistfuls of business cards, copies of their book, bumperstickers, coupons, personalized colostomy bags... whatever. They are promoting the shit out of themselves (reason for the colostomy bags). It's all about them, all the time, and they will try to sell whatever they can. There is also the Social Peddler, they are not at a networking function but in a regular social setting, not trying to sell you anything, yet the conversation is completely one sided with a long winded narcissistic monologue. Oh, wouldya' look at the time... gotta' go.

The Dosey Doe - I will never understand this one as long as I live. They are actively talking to you yet they constantly keep inching to the left and behind you. So every couple of minutes you have to reposition yourself and eventually you've turned around in a full circle. I've tried to figure it out. At first I thought it was to get away from me, but they still keep talking to me. I've even stopped talking and turned my back and they are still talking to my back. Maybe they feel shy deep down and are trying to avoid talking face to face. We could move this conversation to an old fashioned priest's confessional, shouldya' like? Hey if the anonymity would make you feel more comfortable...

There are many more, perhaps to be named later in more adventures. I'm really quite exhausted from having to write about and relive these tiresome creatures. I need a massage, a nap, and a cocktail, or perhaps all of the above...

How I Was Almost a Stripper...

Every time things have been tight (money-wise) or the ex wasn't paying, every would just say "Just get another job!" like it was just that easy.

Well sure, if I had held a job previously as a doctor, lawyer, engineer, executive, or high end call girl, I could have "just gotten another job" again and made enough money to live comfortably and cover day care. However when one has put their career on the back burner to raise children, pretty much the only people that want to hire you are those that need a receptionist for $8-$9/hour, which doesn't even cover child care for 3 kids. And I went to college for broadcasting; they pay about the same as the receptionist job.

So what's a girl to do? Hey, I wanted to work and pull my weight, but I also needed to be a little flexible to care for kids. It's the biggest obstacle for single mothers... how do I make enough to cover daycare costs? And I need an understanding employer for the times I have to stay home with sick kids.

For a few years I had trouble making it work, then I had it figured out being a realtor (working partly from home) for a while, but just as I really hit my stride, the real estate bust happened in Denver. Then years later I moved back here to NY, kids were now in school so I could concentrate on cultivating a career, but the ex disappeared and I was desperate to make up the difference of lost child support. I often heard the phrase, "you could always strip".

Some were joking... some were not.

There were times, very very desperate times, (and a few years ago and 20 lbs. less) I thought about it. For a fleeting moment, I crafted in my head, how I could go to another town nearby where I could perform on stage as "Chrystal Courvoisier" (stripper name + booze = more tips) and wouldn't get recognized by anyone and my kids wouldn't find out. Just make enough to get a little ahead, and BOOM! Problem solved.

We all fantasize about how to solve our money problems - winning the lottery, robbing a bank, selling drugs, waiting for old relatives to die (I didn't, but come on, you know someone has), and hooking. Seriously, who hasn't entertained themselves by thinking "What if?" But like most of us with a shred of conscience, we decide we cannot. If you have kids, sometimes you think you would do just about anything to feed them. I was almost homeless, been that desperate. But it comes down to your... decision. Me, I just could never look my kids in the eye again if I stripped.

I can't label it values, morals, or conscience. I can't judge. I certainly think there are decisions that aren't in yours or the kid's best interest in the long run. But sometimes desperate times call for desperate measures. The survival instinct sometimes brings out rash decisions.

Instead of hooking or stripping, here's what I did... I cleaned friend's toilets for gas money. I swept and hosed down their porches for food money. I helped friends who had businesses, doing menial tasks in order to buy toilet paper. My friends on the internet actually had a small fund raiser for me. I can't tell you how much that helped. I am eternally grateful. I sucked it up and went down to the Department of Social Services and applied for food stamps, heat, and medical assistance. Actually going to DSS to me was more humiliating than cleaning toilets, but I did what I had to do, all until I found a steady job. Or in my case, 3 part-time jobs that equaled 50 hours a week.

I don't claim to be self-righteous. Oh God, not by any means. When my kids weren't around I downed a few gin and tonics and cried myself to sleep. You just do what you have to do. Just stay away from illegal stuff, and keep your adult "acting out" away from the kids. But please keep in mind, there are lots of options before you turn to desperate measures. There are plenty of private agencies to help, as well as the gov't. There is always someone who needs a toilet cleaned. The aid is there, we've paid our taxes and contributed, that's what it's there for.

Don't be afraid to ask for help, it's the most courageous thing you can do for you and your children.

Can a Gynecologist Wear a Clown Suit? (Is Individuality Bad for Business?)

I just saw a Twitter conversation that prompted me to write on a topic. But I've been thinking about this topic for a long time anyway, pretty much anytime I see a makeover show on TV. Oh girl, you just got me started...

At this point in time, in my 40s, you can see what I look like on the front and back cover of this book.

And this is what I looked like in college, circa 1984:

Yea, I was kind of a freak back then, by 1984 standards anyway. I was into punk and new wave music. Into that whole Euro look. I wanted to be Siouxsie Sue of Siouxsie and the Banshees. I was a broadcasting major, into the whole music scene where the Dead Kennedys ruled and hair bands were lame and embarrassing and tres uncool. I suppose I was a hipster before hipsters became a "thing".

I took pride in being an individual. I relished it. Hell, it was a complete cry for attention! Look at me, I'm cool! Oy. I even went so far as to... when I was working at a summer camp, my second year new owners took over and made lots of new rules including "no crazy haircuts". What did Madge do? First thing, got a crew cut and left a long braided tail in the back. What happened? Third year I wasn't asked back.

I started to go for interviews after college in 1987. I was realizing my appearance wasn't getting me any jobs. Yea, I got pissed about "the man" trying to keep me down. Then I quickly realized, I just had to compromise a little because "the man" does run the world, and I'm just a squirrel, tryin' to get a nut... to move your butt. Oh sorry, I was channelling C+C Music Factory for a minute. I digress...

I'm all for being an individual and non-conformist. I was the queen of it. But as I got older I realized, depending on your line of work or path in life, you have to conform a little sometimes. There are a ton of times in business meetings where I want to blurt out "That's what she said!", but I know it wouldn't be professional and I'd probably get canned. Hell, at times you have to downright kiss ass. Oh that one kills me, but hey if I want to feed my kids, sometimes I have to just be nice and to me, bland.

It's been my pet peeve when watching "What Not to Wear". They get a bunch of kooky, out there chicks that have their own style, albeit bad, but it's their "personae". A hippie, a geek, a Goth, a turtle lady, a disco queen, whatever. And by the end of the show, every single one of them looks like a Banana

Republic clone. I HATE THAT! I'm all for dressing someone up, giving them some better fashion tips, especially when it's just to buy stuff that fits! But let them still have their individuality, as weird as it may be.

It's the same with dating shows. They find some weirdo who can't get a date. The first thing the mentor says is "don't be such a weirdo" in order to get them to appeal to a broader audience. But what if your dream match is another weirdo? I mean, I found the same thing when I was dating, I had to be more... middle of the road, more mass appeal, as I said. Is that false advertising? Or does it just give you an entree' to lots of different worlds where you can then open up and be more yourself. Or is your true self just too weird for anyone to take?

It's such a fine line. To look and act presentable and professional, someone people want to do business with or date or be friends with but let them be individuals. Are you not being true to yourself or are you giving yourself more opportunities? I think that's why I don't want to get married again, so that I can be a classic, sophisticatedly coifed professional by day and come home at night and wear Kleenex boxes for shoes and dance to Joy Division wearing just men's boxers and a bra made of rubber duckies. I wish I didn't have to care what people think. I gotta' be me... I just have to pick and choose the times I do it, I guess.

Well There's Always Work in Fetish Films, Right?

I'm in a funk right now. No, not like George Clinton and Parliament Phunkadelic (I wish)... more like "What kind of funk did I just stick my hand in between the stove and the wall?".

I have reasons to be incredibly joyful like taking my son to NYU for his freshman year this weekend. I am so proud, but I think under the surface I have all kinds of emotions boiling - sad (obviously), mad/stressed/overwhelmed (that I have to coordinate and pay for everything myself), nervous (just a little, but he's smart, I don't think he'll get mugged or alcohol poisoning, knock wood, oh Jesus hope I didn't just jinx it).

But I also have legitimate reasons to be in a funk. I can't quite seem to get where I want to be career-wise. I'm kind of at a cross roads with my career. Sometimes I feel I'm on the cusp of greatness, other times I feel like, "Can I just get a God damn break for once?" I've been in survival mode since my divorce 12 years ago, in dealing with an unpredictable ex . So, I've had to take jobs, any job I could find. Sometimes you just have to. But now I'm trying to have a career. Trouble is, I don't have the financial luxury of cherry picking gigs. But in this past month I've turned a corner... and I'm not sure I am comfortable with it.

See, life would be much easier if I was a sociopath or a doormat. I've been trying to speak up at the right times and stay quiet at the right times. And I over-think the shit out of stuff. Last week I quit a job that I just started about 4-5 weeks ago. I had a bad feeling when I got hired but ya' know I did that whole "I need to pay the bills" thing. And I went against a vow I took years ago to never work for a small start-up or non-profit again. Just too unstable and too much red tape and budget constraints. Sorry, but I hate it. I've gotta' get stuff done and get it done now, not fill out 10 forms and wait for a board vote before doing it, only to find out there's no money to pay me.

I don't want to tell too much but it was a place that was very very small (4-5 employees) and was in transition. Danger Will Robinson! Some stuff went down (that involved someone screaming at me abusively) and well... I quit. I have never done anything like that in my life. I do things properly, stick it out, try to work it out, or at least resign properly with a two-week notice. But I had seen some bad signs, trust me and I vowed to never put myself in that position again. (me and my vows)

And of course the Catholic guilt went into overtime. Quitter's remorse. I should have just kept my mouth shut, I need the job, I shoulda' woulda' coulda'. See, here I go, second guessing everything.

My point is... I'm in limbo with what I will take and what I won't. I've discovered before that what you surround yourself with or what you accept is what you get. I guess I need to start accepting better things. BUT, I have 3 kids to support all by myself. No husband, no child support. Me, myself, and I. Kinda' hard to do on shitty $10/hour jobs, but if I don't take the $10/hour, I've got... nothing. Sooooo... therein lies the problem. I keep getting told I have great skills but lack certain specific experiences. I've been making silk out of sow's ear for years now, I'm a little freakin' sick of it. And I'm a jumbly mess of funk. What's a girl to do?

There's always work in fetish films, right?

I don't know what to do about the job thing right now. But ya' know what I would do about crappy situations? Ok here's where I go into dream sequence... I know we all have those fantasies about what we would like to do in real life situations.

Here's what I would do if money and jail time weren't an option...

* I would tell that woman she wears crappy bras and her size J chest doesn't look attractive sitting on her lap and then stab her with a pencil.

* I would kick that abusive guy in the sack and tell him his ideas suck and he should stick to his profession and get help for his OCD and self-loathing issues.

* I would send all the texts with requests for nudes to that guy's girlfriend.

* I would scream "Shut up, shut up, shut up! Nobody wants to hear about your stupid nerd kid all day!" to that lady, ok well several ladies I know. You're not the first person to ever have a child, and no he's not the coolest thing ever. I try so hard to keep talk of my kids to short mentions, not day long commentary at the office or every freaking FB post, Tweet, or blog. Sorry girls.

* I would sue the crap out of that landlord for all my stuff being destroyed by mold and for being an abusive slumlord. Oh and perhaps bash them with a shovel too.

There is such a long list, but alas they are just fantasies I whistfully play in my head to bring a smile to my face. But like in a Wile E. Coyote kind of way not a "Saw IV" kind of way.

I really don't have anger issues, really. I just have an active imagination. By the way, I don't condone violence or destruction of property in any way, but it's fun to envision as if it were a scene in an obsurd quirky cinematic comedy.

The jury is still out on "get whatever job you can" or "only accept good things for yourself." I suppose taking one while you wait for the other is an option, but that has usually just trapped me in an endless cycle. The saga continues…

6. Identity

This section comes after the dust settles and all your crises have seemed to subside, you have to figure out what comes next? Heck you don't even have to go through a crisis to attempt to find yourself, who you are, your identity. (Not the kind that someone steals and runs up your charge card, but what's inside. You could wake up suddenly and realize you don't know who you are or don't like who you are.) You may have been busy raising children for years and just lost yourself. Whatever the case may be, you need to figure yourself out.

Most of these essays were written after a long hiatus of not writing. I was in transition mode and had to regroup. I was headed in a different direction than my previous writing. I wanted to be headed in a different direction than before because the last direction sucked. This post is simply explains that revelation.

Becoming a Functioning Human Being 101

So, I just had a birthday. Back in the olden days when TV only had 3 channels, they would have called me "middle aged". No one uses that term anymore; it's become somewhat of a leper of age classification terminology.

I haven't written anything of any relevance in about a year and a half. I've written maybe 2 or 3 things in that time on a website that nobody gives a rat's ass about anymore. None of those articles were anything interesting anyway, they basically relayed the message that I was still alive. As I also inform you today, I am still, in fact alive.

You may (or may not) ask what my birthday and the thing I've written have in common? A lot. My physical life has been in "manager trainee" mode and my writing life has been "closed for remodelling". The fact of the matter is, I've changed. I'm not the same person I was 1.5 years ago. I picked myself up by my bootstraps and become a productive member of society (not that I really wasn't before), and decided to embark on a career and not just a job. Another factor is that I've gotten into a serious relationship with a man over a year ago. So, you see I've gone from a cynical, man hating, down on her luck, small child rearing, job hopping broad, to a positive, man loving, working her way up, college bound teen rearing, career minded woman. ...what the hell am I supposed to do with all that?

Therein lies the problem. Who am I? Written words flowed out of me like blood from a jugular vein when I was miserable. Words also flow when I'm feeling raunchy and funny, but that's not conducive to being professional (alledgedly). So, how do I write for who I am now and what I want to be? My rather lame answer to that at this moment is... stay tuned and find out.

Ok, ok, I'm sorry! Rome wasn't built in a day, neither was Joan River's face, so we have a bit of a row to hoe. I hope to keep my writing going regularly from here on out with loads of Madge witticisms and tons of my mistakes and triumphs so that my life may serve as an example of how to narrowly avoid ending up as a trainwreck. Oh yes, stay tuned...

A New Reality Show Based on My Cleavage

I don't know about you but I'm really freakin' sick and tired of total useless toolbags or dimwits being rewarded with TV shows, fame and money... just for being complete asshats!

I've been doing a lot of research while planning my next steps to ~~take over the world~~ refine and advance my career. Looking at what's trending, figuring out how to brand myself. Have you seen what's out there? Jesus, Mary and Joseph it's a sea of vapidity, shallowness, low IQs, boorish low class behavior and violent personalities.

It seems the United States has set the bar incredibly low for entertainment and celebrity. I know there have been thousands of blogs and articles and commentaries on all the craptastic useless reality stars and their low rent television shows. But it goes for all forms of entertainment - TV, radio, books, magazines, blogs, theater.

All they do on these TV shows is feature incredibly dim people like Swamp People and Here Comes Honey Boo Boo, so we can laugh at them. Which honestly I think is a little mean, but obviously the dim bulbs don't care as long as they are getting a paycheck. Or they feature scantily clad ladies with bodies made by Mattel, engaged in picking dates or pulling hair (I don't even know what the plot of that Bad Girls Club is other than to have cat fights). Or they show ridiculously rich people with their horrendous problems like so and so didn't invite so and so on the girl's trip to London. F you! That's a major traumatic problem in your life? I'm insulted. Try my life, ya' twatmonster, you wouldn't survive.

Books - "Fifty Shades of Grey"? Really? Do you realize how terrible this book is? Dickens, F. Scott Fitzgerald, and Hemingway are probably rolling in their graves. Not written. And as a mature adult woman, I find the characters extremely offensive. I don't know if offensive is the right word. But the girl is everything that's wrong with women, and he's a controlling douchecopter. Having been married to one, I see nothing sexy about this at all and it's the kind of thing that leads women to thinking it's sexy and adventurous to get involved with a bad boy. Ok, not a bad boy, just an asshole.

Blogs? Don't mean to sound like I'm better than anyone, but some of y'all just ain't funny. Probably not anyone that reads my blog, because you all are smart and have good taste. Ahem. But I've seen some of the really popular blogs and it's just not funny, and the readers are acting like it's the most outrageous hilarious stuff ever, like when the blogger calls herself a hot mess. Ok that term was so 5 years ago. These people probably still laugh out loud to episodes of "Full House" and write ROFLMFAO to "I can haz cheezburger" memes. (Some are worth a chuckle, but c'mon) Did I even write that acronym correctly? I've never written it before in my life.

Theatre - "Bring It On, the Musical"? The cheerleading movie, really? Enough said.

So yea, I'm jealous. Envious, jealous, whatever it takes. I've worked hard, raised 3 very smart kids on my own after their Dad took off, and I work a few jobs. I don't want to be poor anymore, I want that big paycheck. I want to meet Andy

Cohen! I want to have a makeover and be dressed by a stylist. Fuck yea, you bet I do! So, what can I do?

I need an angle, a gimmick, something to brand me. No I don't want burning metal on my flesh, I mean to package and advertise me, make me a brand name. What have I got that's special? Humor? Well maybe, I don't know, funny to some, not funny to others. I'm mature yet hip? Maybe, but I'm not uber hip, I couldn't critique club DJs for Rolling Stone or anything. I'm not gorgeous, not hideous, but not gorgeous. But I have been told I have a nice rack. Even by the select few that have seen me naked said I have the boobs of a 25-30 yr. old (hey at 47 that's a huge compliment) even after having 3 kids! And yes, they are real. My secret is, I didn't get them until I was about 40, they haven't had time to sag. Well, maybe I had them before, I just didn't notice, I was modest. I gained about 15 lbs. and suddenly got ample bosoms. And I have amazing bras. You have no idea what a good bra can do.)

So, that's it. I will try to pitch every media outlet in the world to get a reality show for my rack. A rack could have a reality show, right? I mean, most shows are just about looking at racks anyway right? Just cut out the middle man, don't need vapid girls with dumb premises, just feature my rack. "Madge's Rack".

Oops, need to lighten it up, too emo, too much face in that one...

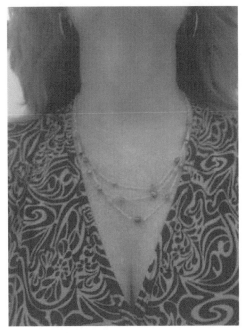

We could feature my boobs on a nice night out, a wacky date or something (too much plot?)...

My rack is even religious and attends church...

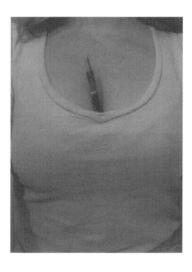

We can show my rack at work, writing...

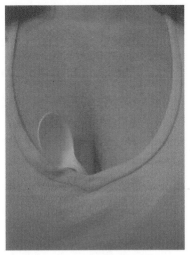

We can show my rack eating regular meals...

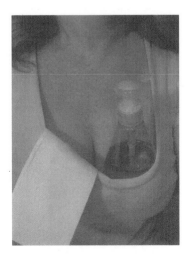

Take a look at my rack doing daily housework...

Look at my rack, it's ready for a formal event!

And my rack, in a highly dramatic plot twist... oh I forgot there are no plots in my show, well maybe a little...

I'll have to throw in some sort of plot to keep the audience coming back because who wants to just look at boobs all the time?

It will be high drama, with tit-ilating dialogue. And then...

I'll throw in something completely different once in a while so that the low brow folks have something to laugh at and relate to...

Well there ya' have it. My new show, featuring my brand... my rack. I could also write blogs, books, and radio shows centered around my rack. Whattaya' think . Just waitin' for those offers to roll in now...

My Name Ain't Baby, it's Ms. Madigan if You're Nasty

I just stopped at ye olde gas station/convenience store combo. I needed a Starbucks Mocha Frappuccino and CVS wasn't open yet. A woman has needs. Anyway, I had just dropped my girls off at school and I was decked out in my finest pajama bottoms, Uggs, Columbia jacket and top knot on my head. I exchanged a chuckle with the nice 20-something young man clerk when I went to pay $2.69 mostly in change. (we broads don't empty our pockets like the guys every night, we collect that shit like lint, I needed to get rid of it) And over the course of the conversation (at beginning and end) he called me "darlin'" twice.

Now... what will Madge's reaction be?

I kinda' liked it.

It was cute. He was harmless. It wasn't forced, you could tell he probably calls everyone that. And the fact that he called a woman probably 20 years older than himself that was just, I don't know... cute. Charming.

I know not everyone likes that. That's the funny thing about pet names or terms of endearment or whatever. A 70 year old woman I know from the country club would have probably cursed the kid out as she feels she deserves more respect. I don't know, at my age (probably her age too) I'd rather be called darlin' than ma'am.

However, we all know there are times when it just feels different. Say when the lecherous old man at the bar keeps calling me "sweetie". I'd be all up in his grill like "I ain'tcho sweetie!" Nah, I'd just walk away 'cuz it was creepy.

Or when the condescending woman at the jewelry counter called me "honey". Oh I felt a big old "fuck you" welling up from my toes on that one. But I held my tongue. See, because if I had gone off on her, I would have proved her theory that I was some low rent broad coming in tryin'a be all fancy. So, to be bitchy I called her "ma'am" when she appeared to only be about 38. heh heh heh I could see the pissiness come over her as I smiled politely. Meow!

As for the men in my life I can't say that I've ever had any concrete pet names from them, unless you count "Mom". And that was from my son, don't get all pervy on me. Actually when my son is being affectionate and not the "I'm far superior to you because I am a college Freshman in New York City and hobnobbing with the world's elite" guy... he calls me "Mum" in a British accent. I like that a lot. Or "Soopah Mum" (super mum) which is a "Shawn of the Dead" reference.

My ex-husband called me "honey". Big deal. My current man calls me... nothing. I think he would beat my annoying ass with a stick if he could instead of calling me a pet name.

I knew a couple that called each other "babe" constantly. It was literally ever other word, "Babe should I use more salt, babe? Babe, what do you think, more salt babe?" Jesus Christ, what are you trying to prove? Get over it, we know you two are together, we're not immigration and you're trying to prove your marriage isn't just a green card scam.

Oh and as one myself I can tell you without a doubt, redheads don't care to be called "carrot top" or "fire crotch". And if you don't know me, don't ever ever yell "hey Red!" at me, or I'm gonna' give you some fire in your crotch with a stiletto heel. As an aside if you ask me if the carpet matches the drapes, you'll get a fork in the eye... or I'll just publicly humiliate you and ask you if you shaved just the middle of your balls to match your hairline.

We women call each other names sometimes. I have a bunch of friends that we called each other "hooker" all the time. That was fun, but got old I guess. It was the funny thing for women friends to call each other "bitch" all the time. I think that's pretty stale too. When I lived in North Carolina in the late 80s I had a girl call me ... I don't know how to spell it. Phoenetically - "shoog". But you know, the first syllable of "sugar" but drawn out. It was quaint at first, but after a while I was like "ok honey the audition for Hee Haw is now over, you can stop".

Dudes, I can't figure you all out. You will call each other the most vile things as terms of endearment. My ex-husband and his friends used to call each other "cocksucker" all the time. "Hey what's up cocksucker?!" Um yea. Then there was "fuckhead", "douchenozzle", "dickhead", and "zoobutt". But they were all hockey players so maybe they were in a class by themselves. I don't know, does that make you all feel closer? Hug it out, shithead!

I guess it's all in the way you say it. I remember having a waitress at a diner locally but she had a thick Pittsburgh accent. She called the guy I was with and me "hon", but it was like every other word. Seriously. Ok, the part of Flo from Mel's Diner on "Alice" has already been cast, you can cut the shit now. It was just really forced and phony. More annoying than charming.

Has anyone ever called you a pet name you absolutely hated? My Dad and certain siblings called me "Peanut" when I was young because I was so tiny. I hated it at first but came to like it more as my ass grew bigger after puberty. Yea, feel free to keep calling me that...

Whoopsie, Pull Down Your Social Media, Your Crazy is Showing...

I try so hard to make sure what I post on Facebook or Twitter isn't annoying. Really, I do. But ya' know, inevitably someone will think I'm annoying. One man's hilarious is another man's "she annoys the crap out of me" What can you do?

But I try hard to avoid the clichés that people most often complain about like:

1. The food report "Making meatloaf and mashed potatoes for dinner. Yum!"

2. The whine "Day 2 of being home sick, oh I feel so terrible and wish someone would make me soup"

3. The health overshare "I just got home from the doctor, still can't figure out what is wrong. Still have purple ooze coming from my rectum. But doc said my mologium levels are normal. Will test my saliva tomorrow"

4. The subliminal message "Some people just can't stop talking about me can they? You better check yourself bitch, I'm on to you."

5. The man/woman scorned that makes you look like an idiot post "I just had a man tell me I'm needy and dump me. I'm sorry I just want to know where you are all the time, it's in case I need you or you might do something bad. Sorry you can't handle my love, jerk. I'll find a real man who can."

6. The boring cliche post "Oh Mondays"

7. The inspirational quote "When Life Gives You Lemons... at Least You Won't Get Scurvy!" oh wait, that's the title of this

book! But that has a funny twist, a boring one would be "God only gives us what we can handle"

8. The uneducated rant "Yea, this country is going to hell because all you Liberals need to have your front wheel drive shopping carts. You know they gave us a new tax on that, didn't you? We need to take our country back!"

9. The desperate grab for attention "Look at my 8,000th selfie that looks like all the others!" or "Hey, I'm running through the house naked" - oh wait that was me.

10. The boring ass Happy Birthday wish "Happy Birthday!" You can't even mention their name? Could you be any more lazy or uncreative? (I may have done this in a hurry, sorry)

So these things I find humorous and try to avoid. The one thing I've tried hard to avoid (since I think I have already done it about 8 years ago on MySpace) is the public descent into madness. Oh I was riding the "the world hates me" wave hard a few years ago.

"Caution: Whacky Post Crossing"

I've seen this person lately who is someone I've only known online for a few years. This person was always a little, I don't know, just not very bright but always doing cocky flirting. Trust me, you have nothing to be cocky about. Not to be a bitch but, this person can't string a cohesive sentence together with more than 2 words spelled right. They boast of being an uneducated redneck. Ok, knock yourself out.

But recently this person has posted several times a day about how we will soon need to retreat to survivalist bunkers and stuff about NY State gun laws will soon be taking our children as wards of the State and putting them in work camps. The twist is, this person thinks they could be the savior. They don't know how these overeducated "experts" can't figure everything out but he/she can. Yes, perhaps we should have a person with 14 kids out of wedlock that can't hold a job, drinks all day, and can't spell "cat" to fix the country. This person doesn't even know the branches of government or how a bill becomes a law. (I recommend Schoolhouse Rock for that)

There's nothing we can do. I've tried to leave the casual "So and so, calm down, concentrate on your family then help fix us" or something nice but rational. It seems to get them riled up and the country needs them even more. And the person's friends seem to goad them on. Like yea "So and so for President". It's like dumb and dumber.

I've also seen the person that is being driven mad by their own paranoia of the opposite sex. This person is totally convinced all opposite sexeses (yes I made that up) are evil. Everyone cheats. Um maybe people just keep telling you they are in a relationship to get you away from them because you are crazier than a shithouse rat and are uber creepy?

It could just be something they're going through, but it could be a serious mental health or substance problem. Who knows?

What should we do when we watch somebody taking the express bus to crazy town in a very public way on social media? Or if somebody is riding the Bitter Bus like it's the bus in the movie "Speed". We can't stop it or we'll die! (Someone please tell me if I exhibit these behaviors so I can eject immediately...) I guess I suggest a private message to tell them that their crazy is showing is in order. Watch my inbox fill up now...

The Culture of the Attention Whore

"In the future, everyone will be world-famous for 15 minutes." I know it has become cliché' and everyone has said it, but yea, Andy Warhol was right. Then some dude named David Weinberger said, "On the Web, everyone will be famous to fifteen people". That's more like it.

With so many different ways to communicate instantly and so many different media venues, and recording devices at our fingertips, fame has become an epidemic. On smaller levels, I don't even know if it's fame... just attention. I had no freakin' idea there were so many people in this world that didn't get enough hugs as a child. There are a whole bunch of people in this world that make strippers (those most in need of attention) look like reclusive loners that think Ted Kaczynski was a social butterfly.

Case in point, a recent non-celebrity attention whore.. Sister-girl goes and files suit that little ole Justin Bieber fathered her child. My guess is, she just wants her 15 minutes (and a little walking around money) anyway she can get it. Even if it's making herself look like a trollop. Have you seen her pics? Ew. If it were true, I certainly hoped he'd have better taste than that. But I guess some guys get a thrill out of slummin' it, too. (read: Tiger Woods)

This may be a dated reference but it's an excellent case study in attention whoreism, that idiot Balloon boy Dad. He doesn't even merit a name mention. Who orchestrates that nonsense and tells your kids to lie just to get his rejected-actor-ass on TV? He should be renamed "D-bag Dad".

How hungry for attention have we become as a society? Is it because there are more chances for fame and money? Is it because people have become less loving? Do we all just need a group hug and a Snuggi? Is it because life has become so stressful and expensive that we have "quick buck envy"? We figure if Snooki can make money, so can we? Oh Christ, if she can, I should be a skajillionaire with my drunk-ass shenanigans. So, I'm 20 years older than her, and my cans are a cup size smaller, it could still happen.

I admit sometimes I find myself in attention whore mode. I wrote an almost daily blog for years with thousands of readers and hundreds of comments each day. That can certainly be addicting. But I stopped. I don't know why. Got writer's block, got tired, started getting haters, whatever. Maybe I just got comfortable with myself.

A couple years have gone by and I find myself dipping my toe into the attention waters from time to time. Posting statuses on Facebook, witty retorts on Twitter, guest blogs for the famous and fabulous. And sometimes when no one responds to my witty retorts... I post a pic with cleavage. There, I said it! Ya' got me! I'm a closet attention whore! I need hugs! Forgive me Father for I have sinned...

At least I admit it, knowing what you are and what you do is half the battle of figuring yourself out.

They also say the first step is admitting you have a problem. I'm Madge, and I'm an Attention Whore.

I'll Be The Old Woman Carrying Booze Around In a Hot Water Bottle

I'm a freak. Always have been, always will be. But I like it. No, I really love it. Sometimes I forget that I'm a freak and I have to go back to my roots and things I love to remind myself.

I went to New York City this weekend to take my son to college at NYU. I'm beginning to think that him going to NYU is going to benefit me every bit as much as it will him. I feel alive. Incredibly alive when I go to the city. I was born and raised near Buffalo and then lived most of my adult life in Rochester (minus 6 years in Denver). I've been going to NYC since I was a kid. My Mother's family all still lived where my Mom was raised in the Philly/NJ/NY triad. Then during the summers when I was in college in the early/mid 80s, I worked at a camp in Western Massachusetts and we would spend all of our days off in NY. Believe it or not, I was one of those Uptown meets Downtown kids hanging out in Washington Square Park with a boombox. I was always a punk/new wave/fringe kid that could also don the pearls for a sorority soiree'.

Now my son is going to school on Washington Square Park. And funny, going there now and looking in the stores, the 80's are back in. Oy. I'm having flashbacks. I never thought this would happen to me in a million years. Hey, and I never pushed my son to go there, I actually really wanted him to go to Cornell. But, maybe things happen for a reason. No, I know things happen for a reason.

I stroll down the streets of the West Village and I see these women in their 70s that are wearing big funky colorful eyeglasses that look like Jackie O. at the Gay Pride parade. They also happen to be wearing get ups that look like Carmen

Miranda wearing combat boots. I WANT TO BE THAT LADY!

I just want to be quirky and adventurous and intellectual and artsy and hip and eccentric. I'm a little too young to be eccentric and I think I could only get away with the Combat Carmen look when I'm a senior citizen but I want to be an eccentric in training. I want to be a 40 something outrageous Mae West meets Betsey Johnson (a fashion designer known for her whimsical/urban/new wave style). I want to be sexy, sassy, funny, and hip. Not douchie hip like those "Gallery Girls" on Bravo TV that I want to punch in the face, but just like, in the know on what's trending and popular, maybe slightly ahead of the curve, but not pretentious about it. I'll sit in a neighborhood dive bar in the Village and trade funny stories for cocktails. Make no mistake, I get the cocktails, they get the funny stories.

I gotta' be me. I always dreamed of living in New York City. Not sure where that dream derailed. Oh yea, I remember, I made a misguided decision at the end of college. I decided to go the safe route, instead of striking out on my own in the big city. Of course I didn't have a job or money either. I probably could have found some friends to live with. Oh well, what can I do? I took a different path. As kids are getting older, I now have an opportunity to reinvent myself. Maybe not reinvent, just go back to my true self. And my true self involves kicking ass and taking names... mostly those of garage band members and drag queens.

So... round two. Maybe I get another chance to be true to my heart and soul? Maybe I get another chance to be outrageous? I have friends in the art world. I have friends in bands. I've been trying to slowly build my wardrobe back to eclectic. I'm happy I got back to my roots and found some black and bedazzled cat eye sunglasses, that was my trademark back in college. Ah if only I had money... Looks like it's fetish films for me, right gang? Give me enough vodka and I can do it! Fact is, I just need to get back to me somehow.

But this time I do things right. This time around I will write more and find more career opportunities, I'll get drunk but I won't get that drunk, I won't sell myself short with men, and I will have more confidence, self- respect, and calculated drive. Don't get any ideas, I wasn't a drunken lazy whore in my youth, I just uh well you know made a few poor choices along the way. Shit happens. *nervous laugh*

I keep telling my kids "You have to make things happen". When they whine about "Nobody is calling me to do anything.", I tell them "Then you need to get on the phone and initiate an activity, try to get a group together to go to a movie or something". If they whine about not being selected for things at school or having trouble in a class, I tell them to go talk to the teacher, ask them what you did wrong, and what you can do going forward. Don't just sit back and wait for the universe, get off your tush and grab the universe by the shirt collar and say, "Hey, I'm over here pal, where are we goin'?!" Well it's time to take my own advice. So watch for me, I'll be the famous writer lady in Doc Martens with a fruit bowl on her head. Ay dios mio... hey ho, let's go!

How Not to Have Your Obituary Read: "She Was a Pain in the Ass"

I've done a lot of reflecting in the past 2 days. One of my best friends from childhood died on Sunday from breast cancer at the age of 46. We first met in kindergarten at St. Mary's School. We made First Communion together and later double dated to proms together in HS and drank in bars together in college. We weren't as close as I would have liked in our adult lives but she lived in South Carolina and I lived in Denver and now NY State. But we did keep in touch.

Anyway, she was awesome. She was always the prettiest and smartest girl in the class. The boys used to follow her around drooling, but she was never vain and she was always nice to everyone. She even befriended the less desirables. She wasn't perfect, she had some trials in her adult life, but everyone still regarded her as a very kind, loving woman.

Which brings me to the point to which I arrived. I was reading her Facebook page and a condolence book attached to her obituary. Many people were writing tributes to her. All of them stated what a warm, kind, loving, caring person she was. That made me think... what do I want to be remembered for?

I know a lot of people who would want to be remembered as a great athlete, great leader, business mogul, mover and shaker, great tan, big schlong... whatever it may be. Without much hesitation, my decision was that I want to be remembered for being a loving person and making people laugh. Not in a vain way, but because all people should laugh and be happy. I want to spread the fun and joy. Let's all have a laugh; it makes the world a better place. I bet all my old time readers didn't think I was such a softie, eh? Yea, bite me...

And the loving part? I'll give you the shirt off my back, but I want us all to respect each other and ourselves too. I love everyone, but a key part of love is respect. That's why Wendy and I were friends, we didn't look down upon others, we wanted to include everyone. We weren't perfect, we still made fun of someone's outfit in high school, but we would usually try to befriend them and eventually give them fashion pointers. I said we weren't perfect!
The point is, we didn't ostracize people. We weren't saints but we weren't haters or bulliers. I still am not that way, and I teach my children the same principles.

Oh, and I also want to be remembered for being reasonable and fair. I hope people would think, "That Madge always made sense and told it to you straight". I don't know if it would be tasteful for me to have "Madge says: Get your head out of your ass" on my gravestone, but it would be appropriate.

I know it sounds dorky but I always wanted to have "What's So Funny 'Bout Peace, Love, and Understanding?" by Elvis Costello played at my funeral. Seriously. I also want "Danny Boy" on the bagpipes and Dennis Leary's "I'm an Asshole" to be played. Is that weird? I'm just about love, fun, and family. Elvis song = love, Dennis song = fun, Danny Boy = family (the Irish thing). And there better be lots of food, booze, and people laughing and sharing stories there.

Take a look at your life, do you want to be remembered as "she never missed the Kardashian's show", or "He was the most hated man in Rochester because he slept with every woman in town and never called", or "She never left a tip in her life", or worst of all "I don't know what he did, slept and watched porn a lot, I guess"? Don't be that guy or girl.

So, you... yea you! How do you want to be remembered? What traits do you want to be remembered for? I suggest you start living it today, for tomorrow is not guaranteed. I say lovingly and laughingly to you, get your head out of your ass and live your legacy!